Evangelizing

Our Children with Joy

Published by Scepter Publishers, Inc.
info@scepterpublishers.org
www.scepterpublishers.org
800-322-8773
New York

Text and cover design by Rose Design

Library of Congress Cataloging-in-Publication Data

Names: Cooney, Mary, author.
Title: Evangelizing our children with joy / Mary Cooney.
Description: New York : Scepter, 2016. | Includes bibliographical references.
Identifiers: LCCN 2016038385 (print) | LCCN 2016038970 (ebook) |
    ISBN 9781594172663 (pbk. : alk. paper) | ISBN 9781594172670
Subjects: LCSH: Christian education of children. | Evangelistic
    work—Catholic Church. | Catholic Church—Education. | Joy—Religious
    aspects—Catholic Church.
Classification: LCC BV1475.3 .C66 2016 (print) | LCC BV1475.3 (ebook) |
DDC
    248.8/45—dc23
LC record available at https://lccn.loc.gov/2016038385

Evangelizing our Children with Joy PB
978-1-59417-266-3

Evangelizing our Children with Joy eBook
978-1-59417-267-0

Printed in the United States of America

Praise for Evangelizing Our Children With Joy

Vatican II has clearly stated that all of us are called to be saints—the universal call to holiness! Jesus stated with utmost clarity this command: "Be holy as your heavenly Father is holy." St. Teresa of Calcutta expressed it in these words: "Holiness is not the privilege of the few, but the duty of all."

Mrs. Mary Cooney, has penned a spiritual masterpiece for busy Moms of the 21st century in her work; *Evangelizing our Children with Joy*. Her message is clear, convincing and to the point: parents must bring their children to heaven and use all the means possible. Quoting Church Documents, the *Catechism of the Catholic Church*, countless saints, and drawing upon her own experience of Mother of of big family, Mary will inspire modern moms to undertake the daunting but most fulfilling task of making future saints—their own children.

Love for prayer, faith and devotion to the Eucharist, confidence in the Infinite Mercy of Jesus expressed in the Sacrament of Confession—all of these hallmarks of true sanctity are expressed with conviction and unction by Mrs. Mary Cooney.

I pray and hope that millions of Catholic Mothers will read, relish and treasure this spiritual gem.

Fr. Ed Broom, OMV
Associate Pastor at St. Peter Chanel in Hawaiian Gardens, CA and
Author of *From Humdrum to Holy*, found at fatherbroom.com

One of the great legacies of Saint John Paul II is his strong defence of the family since, truly, "the future of humanity passes by way of the family." The title of Mary Cooney's book is significant in that it includes three fundamental aspects which echo what is at stake for the future of the family: children, evangelization, and joy. Our Lord came into this world as a child, born into a family. His life's mission was to evangelize our broken and sinful world. By His death and resurrection He has restored for us the joy of being children of God. Mary's advice given to other mothers, based on her own life experience, with practical yet deep wisdom, is a wonderful testimony to the workings of God's grace.

Fr. Charles Nahm
Personal Prelature of Opus Dei, Archdiocese of Toronto, Canada

I love this book(!) because Mary Cooney 'gets' motherhood: "Feeling inadequate is a wonderful place to begin!" she says. Drawing on the wisdom of Scripture, the Catechism, the Popes, the Saints, and Church history, and packed full of Mary's own personal experience and story, *Evangelizing Our Children With Joy* is a wonderful combination of the lofty and the practical, and is a treasure trove for meditation on God's wonderful plan for motherhood and bringing our children to the Lord. Realistic yet hopeful, spirit-soothing and mission-inspiring, I believe mothers will find Mary's book full of soul-striking guidance, encouragement and spiritual consolation. This will be a wedding present for all my daughters and future daughters-in-law!

Holly Pierlot
Author of *A Mother's Rule of Life*

Evangelizing Our Children with Joy is a lovely book with real spiritual insights pertinent to mothers who see their children as the talents God has given them, and whose goal is to return them to Him with interest. Mary Cooney explains the importance of joy in the formation of children, a permeating joy that comes from "a peaceful conscience, gratitude for God's blessings, and deep trust in Our Lord." Such joy is complete when it is His joy in us. As I see it, Mrs. Cooney's book is primarily about love: God's love for us, our love for Him, and the effect that love has on our families. It is practical, because, first of all, love is the foundation of all we do in our families. She discusses the fruits of that love, such as joy and patience, and how to obtain them. For example, patience grows out of understanding. Mothers need to understand children's sense of time, differences in temperament, personality, gender and the various needs those differences engender. This is illuminating. Additionally, Mrs. Cooney addresses the real troubles life brings to most of us. She shares her own sorrows and shows how one can weave them into joyous evangelization. In my own experience of life this is crucial. Everyone is carrying some cross. Mrs. Cooney gives good, solid, practical advice and excellent resources that will help mothers understand and live their own faith, and pass it on to their children.

Laura Berquist
Founder of Mother of Divine Grace Home School and author of
Designing Your Own Classical Curriculum

Evangelizing
Our Children with Joy

Mary Cooney

Scepter

The joy of the Lord is your strength.
—Nehemiah 8:10

Contents

Acknowledgements

Thank you to my dear husband Chris for your insights, patience, and loving support.

To my parents, Rudy and Virgie, thank you for your encouragement, your ever-ready help with the writing of this book, and above all for your unceasing prayers.

By your holy lives and cheerful example, you are the true models of all that is set forth in this book.

Finally, my deep gratitude goes out to Mike Aquilina.

Thank you so much for your kindness.

Preface

I never meant to write a book. I'm a busy mom with a house full of lively children who are with me all day, every day. Our days are full—full to the brim—with school and sports, chores and music lessons, clubs and play dates. At the end of the day, I'm so tired that I can hardly think. And so, last year, when a spell of insomnia hit, I begged our Lord to help me sleep. Instead, he filled my mind with thoughts and ideas, Bible passages and saint quotes. Thoughts about the vocation of motherhood, the Holy Mass, joy and suffering, and God's love and mercy flitted through my mind for hours each night. This whirlwind of inspiration went on for weeks, until I resolved that I should put these ideas down on paper.

I had just barely begun when personal suffering and a trial of faith put a halt to the writing. I miscarried a baby for the fourth time in just over a year and a half. Grief, loss, and deep discouragement darkened my soul. I grappled with strong doubts, wanting to give up on my faith and on God. Four pregnancies and four losses in so short a time, the hopes and worries, the disappointments and tears, the tempestuous hormones—all of these took a toll on my faith and put a strain on my relationships with those I loved most. I was often moody, angry, impatient, and frustrated with my children. I wanted to be cheerful and serene. I wanted to patient and kind. But each time I failed to act charitably, each time I lost patience with my children or gave into moodiness, my despondency only deepened. Like St. Paul, I lamented: "I can will what is right, but I cannot do it. For I do not do the good I want, but the evil I do not want is what I do" (Romans 7:19).

Fearing I might entirely lose my faith in a loving and merciful God, and half wanting to abandon the work of raising our children to love and serve him, I took up my pen and began to write again. It was an attempt to salvage the remains of a battered faith and a broken heart. I wanted to remember and understand why I believed what I thought I believed. What was the purpose of my life and vocation? Why should I bring my children to Mass when it is such a struggle? Does God really love us, or are we just pawns in his grand scheme? Why should I be cheerful when I feel miserable? Why doesn't he answer prayers? How can I accept God's will when his will is so hard to accept? And how am I supposed to teach my children about God's love when he breaks my heart time and again?

I began with the ideas that had kept me up at night a few months earlier. As I wrote, I began to read and research more stories and sayings from the saints and from the Bible. The words that found their way onto paper soothed my soul like balm on an aching wound. The more I read and wrote, the more our Lord filled my heart with understanding and consolation. He gave me a renewed sense of mission, clear and crystallized. I began to marvel at the power of his love and the depths of his mercy. I fell in love, once again, with the Eucharistic Lord. And I experienced a deep and abiding joy, spiritual strength to sustain me through all the ups and downs of raising a family for the glory of God.

Wherever you are in your journey of faith, and whatever your sufferings and crosses may be, I hope the words in this book will do the same for you. I hope that you find, within these pages, purpose and inspiration, hope in God's mercy and faith in his providence, and a way of navigating through the messiness of motherhood with grace and love. May the Holy Spirit guide you, may our Blessed Mother be with you, and together let us joyfully bring our children to Christ.

1.

Our Mission and Our Children's Destiny

Let everything take second place to our care of our children, our bringing them up to the discipline and instruction of the Lord.

— St. John Chrysostom[1]

"What do you want to be when you grow up?" Ask any child this question and the answer will almost always be someone wonderful and great:

"I want to be a superhero."

"I want to be a famous ballerina."

"I want to be an all-star baseball player."

Children want to grow up to be someone significant and awe-inspiring. Deep in their hearts, they know and believe in their potential for greatness. They dream of doing fantastic and heroic deeds, of becoming people who will have great impact on the world around them. Sometimes we smile indulgently at these "childish

---

1. St. John Chrysostom, *On Marriage and Family Life*, trans. Catharine P. Roth and David Anderson, (St. Crestwood, N.Y.: Vladimir's Seminary Press, 1986), p. 68.

dreams," but God has placed these aspirations on their hearts for a reason.

Our children are destined for greatness, each and every one of them. But let us not confuse fame with greatness. All of our children, whether they lead ordinary or extraordinary lives, are called to exemplary virtue, generous sacrifice, courageous heroism, and above all, deep, enduring love. They are called to be saints. Yes, saints, and saints worthy of canonizing! And you and I are, too! To think that our children are unworthy or incapable of becoming saints is an injustice to their dignity. They are, above all, children of God, whose Heavenly Father has created them in his image and likeness.

This is why Christ can and does say to us, "You, therefore, must be perfect, as your heavenly Father is perfect."[2] Our Lord calls us to strive for the perfection of charity, that perfect love for God and neighbor that is the trademark of the saints. His exhortation is meant for each one of us. As the *Catechism of the Catholic Church* states:

> "All Christians in any state or walk of life are called to the fullness of Christian life and to the perfection of charity." All are called to holiness. "'Be perfect as your Heavenly Father is Perfect.'"[3]

And in the words of St. Josemaría Escrivá, "We have to become saints, as they say in my part of the world, 'down to the last whisker,' Christians who are truly and genuinely such, the kind that could be canonized."[4]

---

2. Mt 5:48.

3. *Catechism of the Catholic Church* (2nd ed.), (Washington, DC: Libreria Editrice Vaticana—United States Conference of Catholic Bishops, 2000).

4. St. Josemaría Escrivá, *Friends of God*, (New York: Scepter Publishers), 5.

Our Lord makes no exceptions. You and I are called to holiness. Moreover, we are summoned to raise our children to lead lives of holiness, too. The longing in our children's hearts to be great people stems from their yearning for God. It can only be truly fulfilled when they answer Christ's call to Christian holiness and love. God has created us to "know, love and serve him in this world," and thus "to be happy with him forever in heaven."[5] This is the purpose of our lives and of our children's lives. When we set before our children this fundamental truth, along with the fact that God has a unique and irreplaceable mission for each one of them, we bring meaning, direction, and joy to their lives.

So many parents today sacrifice immense amounts of time and money because they believe their children have the potential to be major league baseball players, hockey players, or renowned musicians. Parents see some athleticism or artistic talent in their children and are ready to devote hours each week and to travel long distances, spending entire weekends at tournaments and competitions so the children have a chance to fulfill their potential. And yet only a very tiny fraction of all those who seriously aim for such heights actually reach the top.

We must see in our own children not only their potential but also their calling to be great saints. And if we parents are willing to make substantial sacrifices for our children to be sports stars or famous musicians for a few fleeting years on earth, we should be willing to do even more for our children's lives in eternity. Nourishing our children's spiritual lives, encouraging them to develop a

---

5. Bennet Kelley, *The New St. Joseph Baltimore Catechism (No. 1)*, 2nd revised ed., (Totowa, N.J.: Catholic Book Publishing Corp; 1995), p. 9.

deep love for God, and forming their characters for true freedom and happiness should be our mission. Heaven is our goal. And no sacrifice can be too great.

> Parents have the first responsibility for the education of their children in the faith, prayer, and all the virtues. They have the duty to provide as far as possible for the physical and spiritual needs of their children.[6]

It is a commonly conceived notion that merely sending our children to Catholic schools or religious education classes fulfills our primary obligation of meeting our children's spiritual needs. But even if we do go to Mass every Sunday and bring our children with us, it is just not enough. The responsibility to teach them the tenets of the faith, to form their consciences and characters, and to inspire a love for God is so tremendous that we cannot simply relegate it to religion teachers or catechism teachers, no matter how wonderful they are. For on this responsibility hangs our children's eternity as well as our own, and perhaps even the salvation of the people God has placed around us.

It is no exaggeration to say that whether or not we take this responsibility seriously could alter the course of history. "These world crises are crises of saints," wrote St. Josemaría Escrivá.[7] You may think that you are just an ordinary mother changing diapers for the hundredth time, but that child you're tending could be the next St. Francis or, God forbid, the next Machiavelli. He could be the next Churchill or the next Hitler. Your vocation as a mother, as a parent, is exceedingly important.

---

6. CCC, 2252.

7. St. Josemaría Escrivá, *The Way*, (New York: Scepter, 1992), 301.

Woman, how divine your mission,
   Here upon our natal sod;
Keep—oh, keep the young heart open
   Always to the breath of God!
All true trophies of the ages
   Are from mother-love impearled,
For the hand that rocks the cradle
   Is the hand that rules the world.[8]

Besides thinking about what our children could be, let us remember what they are now: children of God. And as such, they are worthy of all dignity, all love, and all the spiritual aid they need to return to their Father in heaven. He has destined them for heaven. By this, I do not mean that they will certainly get there, but rather, that is where they belong and where God desires them to spend eternity. However, they need our help, our guidance, and our prayers. God entrusted our children and the care of their bodies and souls to us. This is a blessing and a privilege, but it is also an enormous responsibility.

Knowing our children's heavenly destiny and our responsibility to lead them along the narrow path of holiness, how do we carry out this formidable task? For it is indeed daunting. Our fallen human nature alone is enough to make holiness a challenge. Our human weaknesses and imperfections, our tempers or irritability, our impatience and perhaps our own lack of knowledge of the teachings of the Church . . . are these discouraging? And then there is that culture of death in which we live. Promiscuity,

---

8. William Ross Wallace, *The Hand That Rocks the Cradle is the Hand That Rules the World*, 1865.

moral relativism, a complete disregard for the dignity and sacredness of human life, and widespread contempt for the Church pervade our society like a pandemic, marring and affecting the lives of even the youngest of our children. And we cannot forget the devil (Yes, there is a devil!), who will attack us and our families personally and relentlessly. He will whisper sinister words of despair, discouragement, and deception. Maliciously, he will throw thorns and difficulties along our paths to holiness. With so many towering obstacles, how can we possibly raise our children to be saints?

Feeling inadequate is a wonderful place to begin, because it allows us to humbly cast our weaknesses onto the mercy of God and place our trust in his strength and grace. When we do so, we can say with St. Paul, "For when I am weak, then I am strong."[9] Sometimes, God asks us to do tasks that seem impossible, if not incredibly difficult, because they give us an opportunity to rely solely on his grace. When God asked Moses to tell the Pharaoh to free the Israelites, Moses cowered.

> And the Lord said to Moses, "Go in, tell Pharaoh king of Egypt to let the sons of Israel go out of his land." But Moses said to the Lord, "Behold, the sons of Israel have not listened to me; how then shall Pharaoh listen to me, who am a man of uncircumcised lips?"[10]

Moses felt completely inadequate. And yet, with God's grace, he was the one who led the Israelites out of Egypt. God gave him the grace.

---

9. 2 Cor 12:10.
10. Ex 6:11–13.

And what about the princes of the Church, the apostles? Who were they? They were uneducated, mostly poor, inexperienced young men from a remote village in a conquered land. Even after spending three years with Jesus Christ, they still often did not understand his teachings. They bickered over who would sit at Christ's right hand. Thomas, at first, refused to believe that Jesus had risen from the dead. And Peter, who was to be the first pope and to hold the keys to the kingdom, denied Christ three times when Jesus was arrested. Peter did this even after witnessing the Transfiguration! Were they "qualified" for the immense task of spreading the gospel to the ends of the earth? Hardly! And yet these were the men whom Christ chose! God gave them the grace they needed, and they changed the world!

The history of the Church gives us many examples of people who were as David before Goliath. St. Joan of Arc was only a simple peasant girl, yet she was called by God to lead the French army against the English in the Hundred Years' War. When Our Lady of Guadalupe appeared to St. Juan Diego and asked him to tell the bishop to build a shrine in her honor, he was convinced that the bishop would not listen to a poor native such as he. Yet his obedience led to the conversion of Mexico. And St. Teresa of Calcutta was a young nun who didn't even know how to light the altar candles, and yet she became the foundress of the Missionaries of Charity.

You see, the only real "qualifications" our Lord needs from us are *love* and *humility*, which are made manifest in our readiness to obey God's will. Do you lack knowledge, experience, or patience? Is your house a mess? Are you disorganized? Are your children constantly disobedient and disrespectful? God will work through all that if you let him. He is the Supreme Artist who can create a magnificent masterpiece with even the crudest of instruments. We just need to be like clay in the potter's hand, docile and trusting in God's loving plan for our families.

When I was in college, a professor of musical composition found an old, beat up, out-of-tune piano that had been shoved aside in a storage room because it was beyond repair. Do you know what he did? Using the cracked soundboard and broken strings to make special sound effects, he composed a wonderful musical piece exclusively for that piano. And all of a sudden, the piano held new value; now it could make distinctive, beautiful music that no other piano could produce.

God wants to do the same with us. He wants to take our brokenness, our sinfulness and weaknesses, and transform them into something beautiful and holy. Day by day, little by little, with incredible love and patience, he does this. He pours out his grace on those who trust in him and lovingly seek to do his will, so they can fulfill the unique mission for which they were born.

In every age, God has given his people the graces they needed. He continues to do so today. We need only to thrust ourselves upon his great mercy and to obey his loving will. God, who is our loving Father, will never give us a task we cannot fulfill or a cross we cannot bear. He does not leave us to wallow in our weakness. He does not abandon us or our children in the darkness of our present age. He does not turn a blind eye to the malicious tactics of the evil one. Nor does he turn a deaf ear to the prayers of those who call out to him for help.

Despite the struggles we do and will encounter, we must never, ever give in to discouragement or despair. At times we may be tempted to think that raising our children to be saints is preposterous, far-fetched, and impossible. On our own, this is absolutely true. But with God all things are possible. God, the Father of Mercy, desires our sanctity and the sanctity of our children far more than we do. He is ever ready to pour out the graces we need to fulfill this awesome task of raising our children to be saints. He has a loving concern for the most intimate, seemingly insignificant details of our lives. He is with us every moment of the day, guiding, inspiring, consoling. Moreover, he has given us the sacraments, blessed fonts of grace, to nourish and strengthen us. And we are never alone. The hosts of angels, the communion of saints, and our Blessed Mother are powerful intercessors who come quickly to our aid whenever we call upon them.

Let us ask our Blessed Mother to bless our vocation as mothers. She understands the joys and sorrows of motherhood more than anyone because she has lived them to the fullest extent. No woman has ever loved or suffered more than she has. We can place our children under her mantle and beg her never to let them stray. We can implore her to carry our children to Jesus while we follow closely behind, trying to imitate her and all her virtues. With the love and protection of our Blessed Mother, we have every reason to guide our children on the path of holiness with great optimism, unwavering hope and deep, spiritual joy. For, as St. Louis de Montfort assures us, Mary truly is "the surest, easiest, shortest and the most perfect" way to Jesus.[11]

---

11. St. Louis de Montfort, *True Devotion to Mary*, (Charlotte, N.C.: Tan, 2010).

2.

In Their Father's House
BRINGING OUR CHILDREN TO MASS

This Bread of the Strong gives me all the strength I need
to carry on my mission and the courage to do whatever
the Lord asks of me. The courage and strength that are
in me are not of me, but of Him who lives in me—it is the
Eucharist.

— ST. FAUSTINA[1]

Our vocation as mothers and our mission to evangelize
our children and enkindle in them a fervent love for
Christ require great courage and strength. The ultimate
source of these graces is in Christ himself, the Holy Eucharist. We need to nourish our souls continually on this
Bread of the Strong. And if we wish to raise our children
to be saints, we need to bring them to Mass often so they
can encounter Christ face-to-face. Bringing our children
to Holy Mass, especially when they are young, is neither
easy nor convenient. Often, it entails great sacrifice. But
if we remember and contemplate Christ's Real Presence in
the Eucharist, we begin to understand that there is nothing

---

1. Catherine M. Odell, *Faustina: Apostle of Divine Mercy*, (Huntington, Ind.:
Our Sunday Visitor Publishing, 1998), p. 93.

better we can do for our children than to bring them to Holy Mass.

"If I gave you fifty dollars to go to Mass tomorrow," said a young priest, "would you go?" Thus began a meditation that has stayed with me since I was in high school. "If I gave you one hundred dollars to go to Mass tomorrow," he continued, "would you go? What about five hundred dollars, or a thousand dollars? Would you go to Mass tomorrow if I gave you a million dollars? Of course you would! And yet, one Holy Mass is worth more, so much more, than all the money in the world. For material wealth is fleeting, but the grace we receive at Mass is treasure in Heaven that lasts for eternity. *Eternity!*"

"And what if I told you that the pope himself was going to be at your local parish tomorrow for Mass? Would you go?" challenged the priest. "I'm sure you would go. And yet Christ, who is infinitely greater, comes to give himself to us at each and every Mass."

The human mind cannot comprehend the infinite power and celestial beauty of the Sacrifice of the Mass. Only with faith can we get a glimpse of the sublime mystery that unfolds before us.

> "I am the living bread which came down from heaven;
> if any one eats of this bread, he will live forever; and
> the bread which I shall give for the life of the world is
> my flesh."[2]

How marvelous, how mind-boggling, how enthralling is the fact that at Holy Mass, Jesus Christ, our Lord and Savior, comes to us body, blood, soul, and divinity! He is there, really and truly present before us!

---

2. Jn 6:51.

In the most blessed sacrament of the Eucharist, "the body and blood, together with the soul and divinity, of our Lord Jesus Christ, and, therefore, *the whole Christ is truly, really, and substantially* contained." This presence is called 'real'—by which is not intended to exclude the other types of presence as if they could not be 'real' too, but because it is presence in the fullest sense: that is to say, it is a *substantial* presence by which Christ, God and man, makes himself wholly and entirely present.[3]

"How many of you say: I should like to see His face, His garments, His shoes," wrote St. John Chrysostom. "You do see Him, you touch Him, you eat Him. He gives Himself to you, not only that you may see Him, but also to be your food and nourishment."[4]

Like a lover who never tires of singing the praises of his beloved, we should never tire of repeating this marvelous truth: that Christ comes to us at Holy Mass and that he is spiritually, physically, totally, and completely present. Yes, he is disguised as bread, but he is really and truly there. And, as if that isn't enough, he gives himself to us to be consumed so that we poor, unworthy and imperfect creatures may be united to him, who is perfect love, and thus be transformed by his love.

Just think: At each Mass, God the Son is obedient to the priest's prayer of consecration. Jesus, Lord of the Universe, disguises himself as a piece of bread, again becoming as little and helpless as when he was a newborn baby in

---

3. CCC, 1374.

4. Fr. Florian Racine, *Could You Not Watch with Me One Hour?* trans. C. A. Thompson-Briggs, (San Francisco: Ignatius Press, 2014), p. 60.

the stable at Bethlehem. What utter and complete humility! And his motivation for this divine "abasement" is love, unparalleled and perfect love.

"O admirable height and stupendous condescension!" marvelled St. Francis of Assisi. "O humble sublimity! O sublime humility! that the Lord of the universe, God and the Son of God, so humbles Himself that for our salvation He hides Himself under a morsel of bread.[5]

In a letter to her cousin, St. Thérèse of Lisieux penned, "Remember, little Marie, that this sweet Jesus is there in the Tabernacle expressly for you and you alone. Remember that He burns with the desire to enter your heart.[6]

St. Teresa of Calcutta also spoke of Christ's love in the Eucharist, saying, "When you look at the Crucifix, you understand how much Jesus loved you then. When you look at the Sacred Host, you understand how much Jesus loves you now."[7]

Are you not moved, greatly moved, by Jesus' tremendous humility and love for us? And then consider the transformative power of the Mass. Jesus unites himself to us on earth so that we may be united with him in heaven for eternity. As St. John Paul II affirmed:

> In order to live man needs food and drink. In order to gain eternal life man needs the Eucharist. This is the

---

5. St. Francis of Assisi, *The Writings of Saint Francis of Assisi*, (Philadelphia: Trinity Press, 2012), p. 126.

6. St. Thérèse of Lisieux, *The Story of a Soul*, ed. Rev. T.N. Taylor (London: Burns, Oates & Washbourne, 1912; 8th ed., 1922). "This electronic edition of the autobiography of St. Thérèse of Lisieux includes much, but not all, of the content of *Soeur Thérèse of Lisieux*, edited by Rev. T.N. Taylorshbourne, letter from St. Thérèse to her cousin Marie Guérin.

7. St. Teresa of Calcutta, *http://quotecatholic.com/index.php/charity-love-peace/mother-teresa-look-at-the-crucifix/*.

food and drink that transforms man's life and opens before him the way to eternal life.[8]

And well before him, St. Thomas Aquinas:

In Mass are contained all the fruits, all the graces, yea, all those immense treasures which the Son of God poured out so abundantly upon the Church, His Spouse, in the bloody sacrifice of the cross.[9]

In the words of St. Padre Pio, "Every Holy Mass, heard with devotion, produces in our souls marvelous effects, abundant spiritual and material graces which we, ourselves, do not know."[10]

Do you feel that you have faults and weaknesses you cannot overcome? Together with frequent Confession, regular reception of the Holy Eucharist will help you tremendously. "Receive Communion often, very often," wrote St. Thérèse, ". . . there you have the sole remedy if you want to be cured."[11]

Blessed Pier Giorgio Frassati advocated frequent reception of the Eucharist:

I urge you with all the strength of my soul to approach the Eucharistic table as often as possible. Feed on this

---

8. Homily of His Holiness St. John Paul II, Mass for 12th World Youth Day, August 24, 1997, https://w2.vatican.va/content/john-paul-ii/en/messages/youth/documents/hf_jp-ii_mes_15081996_xii-world-youth-day.html.

9. Rev. Francis Xavier Lasance, Visits to Jesus in the Tabernacle, (New York: Benzinger Brothers, 1898), p. 357.

10. Padre Pio, http://www.catholicbible101.com/thepowerofthemass.htm.

11. In a letter to her cousin Marie Guérin, who would enter Carmel in 1895 as Marie of the Eucharist, Thérèse of Lisieux encouraged her to banish the scruples that kept her from receiving the Eucharist. (General Correspondence, v.1, translated by John Clarke, O.C.D., 569).

Bread of Angels from which you will draw the strength to fight inner struggles.[12]

Feasting on the Holy Eucharist, spiritually and physically united to Christ, you will be transformed more and more into His likeness. You will find your heart being drawn ever closer to His. And the life of the Holy Spirit in your soul will bear those fruits you so long for: joy, kindness, peace, generosity, gentleness, patience . . .

Remembering that our primary vocation and mission is to lead our children to heaven, we can do nothing, absolutely nothing better than to bring them to Holy Mass as frequently as possible. For then we are literally *bringing our children to Christ*. Each time our children attend Mass, they grow in virtue, grace, wisdom, and above all, love for God.

"What graces, gifts, and virtues the Holy Mass calls down!" rejoiced St. Leonard of Port Maurice.[13] It does not matter if your children are too little to understand what is happening at the Mass. Do you think we understand much more? Our pitiful understanding of the Mass is just the tiniest bit more than theirs compared to the sublime reality of what truly happens. And often times, the only real difference between our highly distracted participation and theirs is that we can be physically still while their young blood makes them fidget. St. Leonard further remarked:

Mass is the sun of the human race, scattering its splendors over good and wicked, nor is there a soul so vile

12. Maria Di Lorenzo, *Blessed Pier Giorgio Frassate: An Ordinary Christian*, (Pauline Books & Media, 2004).

13. St. Leonard of Port Maurice, *The Hidden Treasure of the Holy Mass*, (Charlotte, N.C.: Tan Books, 1890), Ch. 1, Part II, no. XV.

on earth who, hearing Holy Mass, doth not carry away from it some great good, often without asking, often without thinking of it.[14]

If even a "vile" soul receives "great good" from attending Mass, how much more will the pure and innocent soul of a child receive?

I truly believe that young children's very presence at Holy Mass is a prayer; their guardian angels are there, praying and worshipping for them. Moreover, the pure and innocent souls of young children are immensely pleasing to their Heavenly Father. He doesn't mind if they are making little noises or crawling on the pew. God is delighting in their presence and the graces he is pouring into their souls.

From the Gospel of Mark we read:

> And they were bringing children to him, that he might touch them; and the disciples rebuked them. When Jesus saw it he was indignant, and said to them, "Let the children come to me; do not hinder them; for to such belongs the kingdom of God. Truly, I say to you, whoever does not receive the kingdom of God like a child shall not enter it." And he took them in his arms and blessed them, laying his hands upon them.[15]

The disciples were not mean or hard-hearted men. Perhaps they saw that Jesus was tired and along came a group of mothers bringing their lively, noisy children with them. Attracted by Jesus' loving gaze, the children ran up to him and, in the eyes of the disciples, they "harassed" him.

---

14. St. Leonard of Port Maurice, *The Hidden Treasure of the Holy Mass*, Ch. 1, Part II, no. XVI.

15. Mk 10:13–16.

Perhaps two children competed for Jesus' lap, another pulled at his cloak with his grimy fingers, and one planted a kiss on his cheek and rested his head on Jesus' shoulder. Other children pulled at Jesus' hands, and all the while they were all talking to Jesus at the same time, clamoring for his attention, his kind words, and his blessing.

Perhaps some of the disciples wanted to correct the children and parents for this apparent lack of reverence toward the long-awaited Messiah. Perhaps some of the disciples only wanted to calm the noisy chaos. But Jesus did not mind this lack of reverence, for what they lacked in reverence, they made up in love. And he did not seem to mind the affectionate clamor, for he knew that this was how children expressed their love. So he said, "Let the children come to me," and he placed his hands on them and blessed them.

Do not be discouraged from going to Mass because your children are fidgety or your babies are noisy. Our Lord, who has made them that way, longs to draw them close to his Sacred Heart, pouring out abundant graces on their young souls. Of course, there are many channels of grace and many ways for them to receive blessings, but none are as powerful or transformative as those graces that come from the Holy Sacrifice of the Mass. So bring them. Bring them to Holy Mass.

"Babies cry, make noise, go here and there," said Pope Francis. "But it annoys me when a baby cries in church and there are those who say he needs to go out. The cry of a baby is God's voice: never drive them away from church!"[16]

---

16. Homily of His Holiness Pope Francis, San Giuseppe all'Aurelio, December 14, 2014, *https://w2.vatican.va/content/francesco/en/homilies/2014/documents/papa-francesco_20141214_omelia-san-giuseppe-aurelio.html.*

On the Feast of the Baptism of Our Lord in 2014, Pope Francis baptized thirty-two babies in the Sistine Chapel. During his homily, he said:

> Today the choir sings, but the most beautiful choir is the children making noise . . . Some of them will cry, because they are uncomfortable or because they are hungry; if they are hungry, mothers, feed them with ease, because they are the most important ones here."[17]

What a beautiful example of love and understanding toward babies and their parents!

When my children were very young, I struggled with the decision of whether or not to spend Mass in the cry room. On the one hand, I did not feel stressed every time my children made a peep during Mass if we were in the cry room. On the other hand, my children often started running around the cry room, picking up crumbs and dirt, pushing chairs, and talking, talking, talking. Moreover, my little ones were too short to see out of the cry room and therefore had no interest in what was going on outside. I wondered what kind of impression my children were getting about the beauty of Holy Mass and Jesus' unconditional love for them when every time we went to Mass, I took them to a dingy, glassed-in room.

One day, I was visiting a church and I saw a sign on the cry room door. It read:

> Parents, please use this cry room only if your child is crying uncontrollably and you need a place to quiet

---

17. Homily of His Holiness Pope Francis, Sistine Chapel, January 12, 2014, https://w2.vatican.va/content/francesco/en/homilies/2014/documents/papa-francesco_20140112_omelia-battesimo.html.

him/her. We desire your child's presence and your participation at the Holy Mass. Once your child has calmed down, please join the rest of the congregation in the main part of the church.

When I saw that sign, I felt great admiration for the pastor. I believe that babies and young children *do* belong at Mass, in the main part of the church, where they can see, hear, and experience the Mass as fully as possible. For little ones, needing to run to the cry room is as inevitable as teething, but babies and toddlers don't belong in the cry room for the entire Mass. As much as possible, young children should attend Mass along with everyone else, among the congregation. After all, as a very kind pastor used to tell me, "They are in their Father's house."

Last year, a local parish was celebrating a children's Christmas Mass. Of course, since it was Christmas, the church was packed. During the consecration, a three-year-old boy suddenly bolted down the main aisle. At full speed, he ran onto the altar, behind the priest, and over to one side of the church. Frantically, his poor grandfather darted after him, but the boy was too fast. He dashed toward the other side of the church. "Come back!" called the grandfather desperately, but to no avail. The little one sped back up the steps of the altar and again darted behind the priest. Following him, the grandfather stopped only to whisper into the priest's ear, "I am so sorry!" The good-natured priest burst out laughing. Finally, another parishioner was able to block the path of the speedy bambino, and the highly embarrassed grandfather scooped the boy into his arms and carried him back to his seat. At the end of Mass, the priest made an announcement: "To the little boy and grandfather who came running up to the altar, WE LOVE YOU!"

So I urge you again, do not be discouraged from going to Mass because of your children's behavior. I know how stressful it can be to bring little ones to church. Many times I have walked down the aisle to receive Holy Communion thinking, "Well, I can't even remember the readings or the Gospel. I'm frustrated with my kids, and my thoughts are far from holy!" Often, I have half-jokingly told my husband that taking the kids to Mass is a near occasion of sin! But God sees the sacrifices we make, and I believe that the more challenging it is to bring our children to Mass, the more graces our Lord pours out on our families. He knows what it costs us to bring our children to him, and he will reward us a hundredfold.

Do you want to maximize on the graces you receive during Holy Mass, even though you are distracted and stressed by your children? Offer up your interruptions, anxieties, and embarrassments for your husband, your children, the priest, or a fellow parishioner. When your children are squabbling over who gets to sit on your lap, when your back is aching because your thirty-pound three-year-old wants to be carried for the entire Mass, when your toddler spills the contents of your purse all over the floor, place all these little tribulations on the altar to be united with the sacrifice of the Mass. Our Lord will graciously receive your sacrifices of love and pour his graces on those for whom you offer them up. Knowing this, you will feel more patient and serene because each wiggle and whisper becomes a small offering for our Lord.

There are some practical things you can do that may help to keep your little ones quiet. Some children enjoy a little church bag with books, lacing cards, and other noise-free items that they get to use only at church. I have found that there is a stage from about eighteen months to three years when feeding a child one Cheerio at a time will keep the little one sufficiently occupied, at least during the Gospel and homily. Around the age of four, some children enjoy scribbling in a small note pad, and by the age of five, they can usually start drawing pictures of things they see in church: the crucifix, a stained glass window, one Station of the Cross. My five-year-old loves the *Illustrated Children's Gospel* published by Magnificat, which has illustrations in comic-book format. If you read these stories to your children at home, they will enjoy flipping through the pages and remembering the stories. I think the hardest age to deal with is when a child has just learned to walk. The impulse to practice this new skill can't be stopped. Take your new walkers for a good, long stroll before Mass begins, and if during Mass they are still clamoring to get out of the pew, or if they insist on walking back and forth on the pew, take them for a walk in the vestibule or along the side of the church. This stage only lasts for a short time, and remember that Christ is delighting in your child and showering his graces upon him. Lastly, a special treat offered as a reward can be a strong incentive for good behavior in church.

Show your children, by your example, how to be reverent in church. Teach them how to make the Sign of the Cross and how to genuflect before entering the pew. Point out the altar, crucifix, tabernacle, Stations of the Cross, and different statues and pictures, and explain what they are. Teach your children to say short, simple prayers, such as, "Jesus, I love you! Help me to be a saint." Encourage them to be especially reverent during the consecration. You might whisper, "See, there is Jesus in that little host. Yes! Jesus is truly there! Let's thank him for coming to us. Thank you, Jesus! We love you!" Enlist your children's guardian angels to help them be quiet, and ask the angels to help your children feel God's presence and love.

Little by little, your children will learn to settle down in church. An hour is a very long time to sit still when you're little and lively. And just think; that energetic toddler who runs gleefully down the aisle in church could be the next St. Francis Xavier! This vitality, which at the moment may seem inconvenient and uncontrollable, is a gift from God. (I wish I had such energy; don't you?) May our children one day use it for God's glory! And in the meantime, we'll work to be patient and understanding and persevere in going to Holy Mass as often as we can.

3.

The Greatest Gift

EUCHARISTIC DEVOTION

> A thousand years of enjoying human glory is not worth even an hour spent sweetly communing with Jesus in the Blessed Sacrament.
>
> — St. Padre Pio[1]

As our children mature and learn to pay attention to and actively participate in the Holy Mass, it becomes easier for us to attend Mass with them. But now, a new obstacle arises: the plethora of activities, sports, music lessons, and clubs that begin to compete for their time, and our time, too. More and more of these activities, especially sports, are crowding out the Lord's Day. What should be a day dedicated to God and family can easily become a day dedicated to sports, with our "Sunday obligation" squeezed in. How this greatly saddens our Lord, who has lovingly prepared a spiritual banquet for us, a feast to nourish our souls and strengthen our wills. And we want to eat and run!

---

1. Manelli, Fr. Stephano, *Jesus, Our Eucharistic Love*, (Academy of the Immaculate, 1996).

In the face of such temptations, we need to remember our children's true calling: to be saints. Earthly achievements, scholarships, Olympic medals, even winning the Nobel Prize—these things pale in comparison to what our Lord is calling our children to seek: a deep love for God and eternal happiness with him in heaven. "For what does it profit a man to gain the world and forfeit his life?"[2] Of course, sports, music lessons, and other such activities help children develop virtues such as sportsmanship, concentration, perseverance, and attention to detail. And it is for this reason that we enroll our children in these activities. But they must never take precedence over the practice of our faith. Sunday should remain a holy day, a day when we focus on God, giving thanks for all of his countless blessings.

> Remember the sabbath day, to keep it holy. Six days you shall labor, and do all your work; but the seventh day is a sabbath to the Lord your God; in it you shall not do any work, you, or your son, or your daughter, your manservant, or your maidservant, or your cattle, or the sojourner who is within your gates; for in six days the Lord made heaven and earth, the sea, and all that is in them, and rested the seventh day; therefore the Lord blessed the sabbath day and hallowed it.[3]

Notice the length of this text. Only in this commandment and in the first commandment does God give such lengthy and clear detail. He is emphasizing the importance of this commandment, and it is not to be taken lightly. He

---

2. Mk 8:36.
3. Ex 20:8–11.

is our loving Father who knows we need to take time to nurture our relationship with him and who wants to nourish our souls with his Body and Blood.

Remembering the tremendous and eternal value of the Mass, again I repeat: there is nothing, absolutely nothing, better for our children than bringing them to Holy Mass. And not just on Sundays but even during the week, if possible. *What? Are you nuts?* I know, I know; you are busy. Very busy. I'm busy; we're all busy. But I ask you: Is there any activity that could be more beneficial to your soul and to your children's souls than receiving Holy Communion? A half hour at Holy Mass is time infinitely better spent than a half hour spent checking e-mail, surfing the internet, watching your favorite TV show, reading a good book, or shuttling your kids to this activity or that.

Do you remember the story of Martha and Mary?

> Now as they went on their way, he entered a village; and a woman named Martha received him into her house. And she had a sister called Mary, who sat at the Lord's feet and listened to his teaching. But Martha was distracted with much serving; and she went to him and said, "Lord, do you not care that my sister has left me to serve alone? Tell her then to help me."
>
> But the Lord answered her, "Martha, Martha, you are anxious and troubled about many things; one thing is needful. Mary has chosen the good portion, which shall not be taken away from her."[4]

I completely relate to Martha. She wasn't busy working for herself. She was serving Jesus and his apostles.

---

4. Lk 10:38–42.

Feeding thirteen hungry, young men means you have a lot
of food to prepare. Someone had to do the cooking! Like
her, we too can become so busy serving and caring for our
families that we forget the 'better part.' So our Lord calls
us to prayer, and not just to "pray while you work." That
is beautiful and wonderful. But even more, he calls us to
literally be with him, to sit at his feet in prayer like Mary.
And the Holy Mass is the highest form of prayer.

Whenever we feel overwhelmed with the amount of
work that we have to do, recall the story of the multiplication of the loaves and fishes.

> After this Jesus went to the other side of the Sea of Gal-
> ilee, which is the Sea of Tiberias. And a multitude fol-
> lowed him, because they saw the signs which he did on
> those who were diseased. Jesus went up into the hills,
> and there sat down with his disciples. Now the Passover,
> the feast of the Jews, was at hand. Lifting up his eyes,
> then, and seeing that a multitude was coming to him,
> Jesus said to Philip, "How are we to buy bread, so that
> these people may eat?" This he said to test him, for he
> himself knew what he would do. Philip answered him,
> "Two hundred denarii would not buy enough bread
> for each of them to get a little." One of his disciples,
> Andrew, Simon Peter's brother, said to him, "There
> is a lad here who has five barley loaves and two fish;
> but what are they among so many?" Jesus said, "Make
> the people sit down." Now there was much grass in
> the place; so the men sat down, in number about five
> thousand. Jesus then took the loaves, and when he had
> given thanks, he distributed them to those who were
> seated; so also the fish, as much as they wanted. And

when they had eaten their fill, he told his disciples, "Gather up the fragments left over, that nothing may be lost." So they gathered them up and filled twelve baskets with fragments from the five barley loaves, left by those who had eaten.[5]

Imagining this Gospel story, I can just see how some of the disciples looked at the young boy and his little offering and smiled at his naive generosity. How could so meager a meal feed such a large crowd of people? Only a child could make such a foolish proposal. But, moved by compassion for the crowd and by the trusting faith of the child, Jesus took this little offering and miraculously fed the multitude. Can't you just imagine Jesus' loving gaze on this generous, faith-filled child?

I know it may seem excessive to try to attend Holy Mass during the week, especially if you are a busy mother trying to meet the endless needs of a growing family. But that sacrifice of time, and the act of love and trust we make when we come to Mass, is like the five loaves and seven fish the young boy offered to our Lord. What does our Lord do? He takes our small offering and, in return, blesses and multiplies our work and our efforts, making it possible to accomplish what we thought was impossible.

I have seen this happen time and again in the lives of ordinary people who go to daily Mass. I have seen this in my parents and family friends who accomplish much with serenity and grace. I know women who, besides raising their large families, have undertaken several apostolic and charitable endeavors: teaching and organizing catechism

---

5. Jn 6:1–13.

classes, marriage preparation classes, summer camps, girls' and boys' clubs, and Bible studies; some have even founded schools. Where do they find the time, and how do they have the energy? It comes from a prayer life nourished by daily Mass.

St. Isidore gives us an example of how God blesses our work when we give him first place in our lives. St. Isidore was a poor laborer who worked on the estate of a wealthy landowner in Spain. He had a great love for Jesus in the Eucharist. Each day, he would rise early in the morning to attend Mass. Because of this, however, Isidore was often late for work, and so his fellow laborers complained to the landowner. The landowner reproached Isidore, but this did not stop Isidore from going to Mass. When the landowner came to the field the next day, he couldn't believe his eyes. For there was Isidore plowing the land, but beside him were two angels, one on either side, plowing along with him.[6]

Perhaps one of the greatest examples from our time is St. Teresa of Calcutta. How did one simple, humble nun become founder of a worldwide order that, at the time of her death, had over 4,000 sisters? How did one poor, little nun build orphanages, hospices, and homes for "refugees, the blind, disabled, aged, alcoholics, the poor and homeless, and victims of floods, epidemics, and famine?"[7] She did all this through prayer and especially through Mass and Eucharistic Adoration. Every day, St. Teresa spent hours in

---

6. Ott, Michael. "St. Isidore the Labourer." *The Catholic Encyclopedia*, Vol. 8, (New York: Robert Appleton Company, 1910), 1 Jun. 2015 <*http://www.newadvent. org/cathen/08189a.htm*>.

7. Spink, Kathryn. *Mother Teresa: A Complete Authorized Biography*, (New York: Harper Collins, 2011), p. 284.

prayer and Adoration, and she began each day attending Holy Mass. Because of her faithfulness in putting Christ first, our Lord multiplied her efforts and blessed her work tremendously.

> In the example of Blessed Teresa of Calcutta we have a clear illustration of the fact that time devoted to God in prayer not only does not detract from effective and loving service to our neighbor but is in fact the inexhaustible source of that service.[8]

St. Juan Diego also knew the infinite value of the Mass. Every day he would make the long trek from his home to the nearest church, fifteen miles away, on foot. He was a poor farmer and laborer who took upon himself the care of his ailing uncle. It would have been reasonable, given the distance from the church and the burden of his responsibilities, for him to go to Mass only on Sundays. But his faith and love for Jesus in the Eucharist were so strong that he went to Mass every day, despite the difficulties. And what happened? Our Lady appeared to him and miraculously imprinted her image, the image of Our Lady of Guadalupe, onto his tilma. "Within six years of this apparition, six million Aztecs had converted to Catholicism."[9] God had seen Juan Diego's sacrifice of faithfulness and his great love for the Eucharist and multiplied and magnified his prayers and efforts toward the evangelization of his people in a most astounding and miraculous way.

---

8. Benedict XVI, *Deus Caritas Est*, (United States Conference of Catholic Bishops, 2006), p. 46.

9. "Our Lady of Guadalupe," *http://www.catholic.org/about/guadalupe.php.*

The practice of daily Mass is not just for religious nuns and priests or for the retired elderly. St. Juan Diego and St. Isidore were both poor, hardworking, married lay-men. If we look at the lives of St. Elizabeth Ann Seton, St. Zélie Martin (the mother of St. Thérèse of Lisieux), and St. Gianna Molla, we see busy mothers with numer-ous responsibilities who nonetheless made attending Holy Mass their top priority. St. Zélie, a mother of five, ran a lace-making business. Her work was so exquisite that she was the most sought-after lace-maker in Alencon. St. Eliz-abeth Ann Seton lost her husband to tuberculosis while her four children were still young. To provide for her fam-ily, she became a school teacher. She eventually founded the Sisters of Charity. St. Gianna Molla was a young mother and doctor, making house calls at all hours of the day and night, delivering babies and serving the sick and poor. These women were very busy. But they burned with love for Christ, and they knew that the reason for their work, the wisdom to guide their work, and the grace and strength to do their work with Christ-like love and joy all came from the same Divine Source: the Holy Eucharist.

Now let me make myself clear; we do not seek Christ in the Eucharist so that we can be more effective workers or that we may accomplish many things. I only mention this "secondary blessing" because I know that when we are overwhelmed with work, we can begin to think that we do not have time for prayer or Mass. And that simply isn't true. Rather, the more responsibilities we have, the more we are in need of God's grace and the more we need prayer. It would be ludicrous for an athlete running a mar-athon to say he had no time to drink water. In the same way, if God has given us many responsibilities, the more we need the life-giving, invigorating, refreshing grace of the Blessed Sacrament.

When we frequent the sacraments, God blesses our work and transforms our souls; there is no doubt about it. However, we often do not see the transformative graces and fruits of the Mass until we have persevered for years, perhaps even decades. Mastering a musical instrument takes years of study and countless hours of dedicated, focused practice. A child who expects to be able to play Chopin's piano études after only a few years of study will be greatly disappointed. In the same way, if we expect to see great spiritual progress and growth in virtues in ourselves or our children after only a few years of frequenting the sacraments, we may find ourselves discouraged and tempted to give up. Of course, there are spiritual prodigies, just as there are musical prodigies. And, of course, there are moments of extraordinary, life-changing epiphanies and conversions. But for most of us ordinary people, spiritual growth is slow, often seemingly imperceivable, and marked with only occasional growth spurts.

We would not say to a child, "My goodness! I've been feeding you three meals a day and you've only grown an inch this year! I give up! I won't feed you anymore." Yet we can easily think this way with regard to our children's souls. So often I have been tempted to think, "I've been bringing my children to daily Mass for years, and we're still the same rotten old bunch! My kids are still self-centered, and I'm still impatient and moody! What's the point? I may as well give up." The devil wants us to stop nourishing our children's souls. He does this by pointing out our apparent lack of progress, thus attacking our faith in the power of the Mass. But progress is not what's really important. Persevering in love—that is what our Lord really wants.

We need to have faith in the transformative power of the Mass. We need to believe that at each Mass, Christ truly does fashion our souls more and more into His Divine Image. But at the same time, we need to trust that, although we do not see or feel this happening, the Holy Spirit is at work, inspiring and guiding us and our children. We, who belong to the generation of instant gratification, want to see results right away.

Recall the Parable of the Sower:

> A sower went out to sow. And as he sowed, some seeds fell along the path, and the birds came and devoured them. Other seeds fell on rocky ground, where they had not much soil, and immediately they sprang up, since they had no depth of soil, but when the sun rose, they were scorched; and since they had no root they withered away. Other seeds fell among thorns, and the thorns grew up and choked them. Other seeds fell on good soil and brought forth grain, some a hundredfold, some sixty, some thirty.[10]

We want the seed to shoot up while our hearts are yet like the rocky soil. But sudden and rapid progress is often short-lived. Rather, we must patiently wait for the Holy Spirit to tend and till the soil, making our souls fertile ground for the Word of God. Then the seeds will bring forth grain, "some a hundredfold, some sixty, some thirty."

In bringing our children to Mass, we nourish their souls as well as our own with rich and abundant graces.

---

10. Mt 13:3–9.

But we need to be patient and persevere, trusting in God's impeccable timing. More importantly, we should not focus on what we get out of the Mass but on the love that we put into it.

In the end, attending daily Mass is about faith and love. It is about believing in the wonderful miracle of the bread and wine becoming the Body and Blood of Christ at the moment of consecration. It's about believing with strong conviction that Christ is truly present in the Holy Eucharist, body, blood, soul and divinity. Going to daily Mass is about being convinced that he comes down to the altar out of love for you, to draw you closer to him, to be united with you, to flood your soul with grace and make you more and more in His Divine Image. It's about sitting at the feet of Jesus, like Mary, trusting that God will provide for all of our needs and take care of all our concerns.

Above all, it's about love. *Here I am, Lord, because I love You. I want to be with You. I want to receive You into my body and be completely united with You. I thank You for all the blessings You have showered upon me. I know I am unworthy, but I trust in Your unending mercy. I am Yours, and all I have is Yours: my life, my family, my work, my desires, my sufferings, my hopes, and my disappointments. I offer these all to You, to be united with Your offering on Calvary to the Father. My Jesus, how I love You!*

Perhaps you are thinking: *But my faith and love are so weak!* You are not alone. We all feel this way at some point or another. There are two ways to grow in faith: beg for the grace of faith, and act as if you have faith. And there are two ways to grow in love: beg for the grace of love, and act as if you do love. There is nothing our Lord desires more than for you to grow in faith and love. If you sincerely pray for an increase of faith and love, he will surely answer your prayers. But we also need to put in our own effort. If your faith in the presence of Jesus in the Eucharist is weak, go to Holy Mass and Adoration of the Blessed Sacrament frequently. Gazing upon the face of Jesus in the Holy Eucharist, you will find your faith strengthened and your love inflamed.

Some families have a special advantage: the flexibility of their schedules makes it possible to plan each day around Holy Mass. And there is no better teacher than the Divine Master. If only we realized what graces, what wisdom and love our Lord pours into the souls of our children when we bring them to Mass, we would no longer consider it a "sacrifice" but rather a joy, a blessing, a privilege, and a gift. In his *Letter to Families*, St. John Paul II wrote:

> There is no other power and no other wisdom by which you, parents, can educate both your children and yourselves. The educational power of the Eucharist has been proven down the generations and centuries.[11]

If you are willing and able to drive your children to piano lessons, sports, clubs, field trips, play dates, and so on, I encourage you to pray and consider whether or not God is calling you to attend Mass a few days a week or every day with your children. For what will bring them eternal life? Piano lessons or being inspired by the Word of God? Baseball practice or receiving Jesus in the Holy

---

11. St. John Paul II, *Letter to Families*, 2 February 1994. *https://w2.vatican.va/content/john-paul-ii/en/letters/1994/documents/hf_jp-ii_let_02021994_families.html*. 18.

Eucharist? Science club or the graces of wisdom and virtue? *"But seek first his kingdom."*[12] Earthly endeavors pass away. Educate your children for eternity!

And yet, a woman's life is seasonal. There may be times when it is really, truly not possible to get to Mass during the week. Perhaps you have a job that requires you to be at work during Mass. Perhaps you have a newborn who keeps you up all night, and you are utterly sleep-deprived. Perhaps you have a child who is sick. I have had some winters when, for weeks, there was always at least one child sick with a cold or flu. During these times, we can unite ourselves spiritually to the Mass being offered in our local parish. We can, with our children, read aloud the reading(s) and Gospel of the day and reflect on them.

A mother of twelve showed me this beautiful spiritual communion prayer, in which we send our guardian angels to attend Mass for us:

Go, my Angel Guardian dear,
To church for me, the Mass to hear.
Go, kneel devoutly at my place
And treasure for me every grace.
At the Offertory time,
Please offer me to God Divine.
All I have and all I am,
Present it with the Precious Lamb.
At the consecration,
Adore for me the great oblation.

_____

12. Mt 6:33.

Pray for all I hold most dear,
Be they far or be they near.
Remember, too, my own dear dead
For whom Christ's Precious Blood was shed.
And at Communion bring to me
Christ's Flesh and Blood, my food to be.
To give me strength and holy grace,
A pledge to see Him face to face.
And when the Holy Mass is done,
Then with His blessing, come back home. Amen.

Growing up, my parents taught me to pray this short spiritual communion throughout the day:

I wish, Lord, to receive you
With the purity, humility, and devotion
with which your holy Mother received you,
and with the spirit and fervor of the saints.

Spiritual Communions devoutly prayed enkindle our love for the Eucharistic Lord and stir within our hearts a desire to receive him at Mass. During those times when getting to weekday Mass is not possible, they keep our hearts from becoming tepid. We must pray that our hearts never grow cold or indifferent toward Jesus Christ in the Eucharist. Such indifference causes our Lord great sorrow because he knows that the way of apathy leads to the slow death of our souls. Rather, we ought to be like St. Faustina who continually united herself to our Lord:

O Prisoner of Love, I lock up my poor heart in this tabernacle that it may adore You without cease night and day. I know of no obstacle in this adoration, and even though I be physically distant, my heart is always with You.[13]

We should try to stir within our hearts and the hearts of our children a great love and devotion for the Holy Eucharist. Besides going to Holy Mass, visiting Jesus in the Blessed Sacrament and spending time in Eucharistic Adoration will draw us ever closer to him, strengthen our faith, enkindle our love, and draw forth countless graces for ourselves and our families. St. Teresa of Calcutta witnessed this within her own order. Once her sisters began having daily adoration, she noticed a "great change" in her congregation: love that was more intimate, more understanding, and more compassionate.[14] Imitating the saints in this beautiful devotional practice, we press on, inspired by the words of St. John Paul II: "I encourage Christians regularly to visit Christ present in the Blessed Sacrament of the altar, for we are all called to abide in the presence of God."[15]

We are also encouraged by St. Alphonsus Liguori:

True, our Lord hears our prayers anywhere, for He has made the promise, "Ask, and you shall receive," but He has revealed to His servants that those who visit Him

---

13. St. Faustina Kowlaska, *Diary: Divine Mercy in My Soul*, (Marian Press, 2005), Notebook I, 80.

14. Mother Teresa of Calcutta, *No Greater Love*, (Novato: New World Library, 1989) p. 154.

15. Thomas J. McGovern, *The Most Holy Eucharist: Our Passover and Our Living Bread*, (Sophia Institute Press, 2013), p. 120. This is an excerpt from the 1996 letter of Pope John Paul II to the bishop of Liege to mark the 750th anniversary of the first celebration of the feast of Corpus Christi.

in the Blessed Sacrament will obtain a more abundant measure of grace.[16]

And St. John Bosco:

Do you want the Lord to give you many graces? Visit Him often. Do you want Him to give you a few graces? Visit Him rarely. Do you want the devil to attack you? Visit Jesus rarely in the Blessed Sacrament. Do you want him to flee from you? Visit Jesus often![17]

Of course the frequency and duration of our visits to the Blessed Sacrament should be in accord with our state in life. If you have a vanload of young children and you are making a visit to the Blessed Sacrament, you and your children might pray only for a few minutes. As your children get older, they will naturally learn to pray for longer periods of time. How beautiful it is to see a child praying earnestly before the Blessed Sacrament! Children are capable of great love and devotion towards the Holy Eucharist and our Blessed Mother. But such devotion needs to be encouraged and nourished.

When your children are very young, you can tell them, "Come! We are going to visit Jesus, who is in the tabernacle in church waiting for us. Let's thank him for all the good things he has done for us. Tell him you love him. And then tell Jesus anything you want. He will listen to you because he loves children very much." Remind your children to bless themselves with holy water and to genuflect reverently before entering the pew. How delighted

---

16. Lawrence Lovasik, *The Basic Book of the Eucharist*, (Sophia Institute Press, 2001) p. 36.

17. *http://saintbosco.org/quotes/index.php?cat=8.*

is our Lord when you bring your little ones before him in this way! If your young children gaze upon the tabernacle or crucifix for even a minute or two, that is enough! God sees their efforts and blesses them tremendously.

When your children are old enough to read, give them a beautifully illustrated prayer book. Invite them to join you for ten to twenty minutes of prayer in Eucharistic Adoration. It may take a little persuading and friendly cajoling, but keep on trying. "Just think how happy our Lord will be if you spend even ten minutes in Adoration," you can tell your more reluctant children. "He is waiting for you. He knows you would rather be playing. It is a little sacrifice that you can make for him. Come on; let's show him how much we love him! You'll be so happy that you did."

Perhaps your children will join you. Perhaps they won't. Do not force them or make them feel guilty. But persevere in making visits to the Blessed Sacrament and spending time in Adoration as befits your state in life. Persevere in encouraging your older children to join you, and in God's time, they will. And, God willing, they will be drawn to the beauty and peace of God's presence and come back to Adoration time and time again.

I would like to mention two final points. First, going to daily Mass, making visits to the Blessed Sacrament, and spending time in Adoration on a regular basis–these are not spiritual "achievements." Of course they require effort—sometimes great effort—and sacrifice on our part. And our Lord is very pleased with our efforts because they are a sign of our love for him and our faith in his Real Presence in the Eucharist. But we must always shy away from the temptation of spiritual pride, the thought that because we have a devotion to the Eucharist, we are holier than others. Rather, let us always pray for humility.

Going to daily Mass and spending time before the Blessed Sacrament is, above all, a grace that God has deigned to bestow on us, unworthy though we are. If we go to daily Mass, it is only because God has given us the grace of faith, has imbued in us a longing to receive Him, and has removed all obstacles. For this very reason, each time we receive Holy Communion or spend time in prayer before the Blessed Sacrament, we should thank him for this undeserved yet immense blessing. *Thank You, dear Jesus, for letting me come to Mass. Thank You for letting me receive you, unworthy though I am. Thank you for all the graces you bestow on me and my family. With all my being, I thank you, my Lord and my God!*

If you desire to go to Mass more frequently but for some reason find that you just can't make it happen despite your best intentions, pray for the grace to go to Mass. Ask our Lord to remove all obstacles and even to make it easy for you to go. Life can be so unpredictable, especially when you have young children. So many times I have thought I was going to make it to Mass on time when all of a sudden a toddler has a meltdown or a child can't find her boots. Persevere anyway. Much of the spiritual life is simply about perseverance. God will bless you richly for your efforts and your faithfulness.

Finally, unpredictable obstacles, criticisms from others, and feelings of interior resistance to attending weekday Mass are very often the work of the devil. And you can count on him to get in the way. The last thing he wants, of course, is for you and your children to fall deeply in love with the Eucharistic Lord. So he will do everything he can to persuade you that you are too busy or that getting to Mass is too demanding and you should just give up.

Several years ago, I was at a weekday Mass with my children in a very small church. We were sitting in the back pew waiting for Mass to begin when a lady whom we had never seen before entered the church. She looked very perturbed as she glanced about the church and then scowled when she saw us. Yet, she took the pew almost across the aisle from us. I could tell that the woman was unhappy. Her demeanor was restless and edgy, and she often sighed heavily.

"Mommy, why does that lady keep frowning at us?" whispered my five-year-old son.

"Shh! Just say a prayer for her," I whispered back. I was beginning to feel a little anxious because I sensed that the little sounds my children made during Mass would distract the poor woman. And they did. She became increasingly agitated, casting irritated looks at my children.

In the middle of the homily, my one-year-old crawled out of the pew. I was about to pick him up when the lady whirled around and angrily yelled, "Oh, why don't you just go HOME!"

I was speechless. I couldn't believe that she had just yelled in the middle of the homily. Suddenly, my three- and five-year-old sons began pummeling each other. At the same time, my one-year-old smacked his lip on the corner of the kneeler and began spouting blood on the floor and screaming. Quickly, I yanked the two fighting siblings apart and took my crying baby outside to calm him down. Clearly this was the malicious work of the devil, trying to make the Holy Mass stressful and difficult so I would give up and go home.

More recently, I had another experience of the devil trying to prevent us from going to Mass. It was on September 8, the Nativity of the Blessed Virgin Mary. Since it was Our Lady's birthday, I really wanted to attend Mass. But, one after another, obstacles were placed in my way. The children slept in, they dawdled over breakfast, one of my sons was grumpy, and we couldn't find my daughter's toothbrush. Just as it was time to leave, the boys had to change because their clothes were grubby . . . and my youngest son was still lying in bed in his pajamas. It was getting later and later. All the while, I kept thinking that we weren't going to make it to Mass. Somehow, with the grace of God, we made it to the church. The older children ran ahead while I followed behind with my lagging little ones, who were upset because I had forgotten to bring them a book. Just as we reached the doors to the church, I saw, to my utter surprise, a *large, black snake lying straight across the path to the doors.* At first I chuckled, thinking it was a joke. The snake was so large, thick, and shiny that I thought it couldn't possibly be real. But as my daughter stepped close to it, the snake suddenly raised its head, coiled itself up, and started flicking its tongue. I screamed and snatched my daughter, who began to cry. It was as if the devil himself, in the form of a large, black serpent, was barring our way to Mass. On Our Lady's birthday, of all days!

Thankfully, the church secretary was behind us. "It's a black snake!" she exclaimed. "I have a key to the side entry. I'll let you in and then see if I can chase the snake away." Carefully, we backed away from the evil-looking snake and made our way to the side entrance. After Mass, my six-year-old son announced, "Mommy, that was a black rat snake!" He was right. Although I had never seen one, black rat snakes live in Maryland. They can grow to be six feet long. Even though their bites are not venomous, they are painful. I was thankful that somehow my older children had gotten into the church before the menacing creature slithered over the path to block our way. But I couldn't help thinking, *"Really, Blessed Mother? A snake on your birthday?"*

However, Our Lady had a special message for me that day. When we arrived home from Mass, I sent the children out to the backyard to play. I expected them to run around, kicking the soccer ball. But when I looked out the window, they were standing by the back fence looking out into the stream behind our yard. I opened the door and called out, "What's going on?"

"Mommy! There's a baby fawn right by our fence!" A baby fawn? We had never seen deer around our house. I ran out to see for myself, and sure enough, a sweet, little baby fawn lay curled up right outside our fence. It was probably only a few days old, and it lay completely still. I wondered why it did not run away.

"Is it still alive?" I asked the children.

"Yes! It's breathing, see?" said one of the boys.

"Maybe it's sick and abandoned," I thought aloud. "I wonder if we should bring it some water." We watched the baby fawn closely for a few minutes. "Let's call Grandma. She'll know what to do. She knows all about deer," I suggested.

We called, and it so happened that a friend of hers, who was an expert on deer farming, was visiting her. "Its mother is nearby. Leave the baby fawn alone. The mother will take care of her." This was the advice from Grandma and her friend. We looked around but could see no other deer.

"The fawn is by itself, and it's not moving. Are you sure we shouldn't do something?" I asked.

"Yes. The mother is definitely nearby and watching."

So we left the fawn and its unseen mother. A few hours later, one of the boys went out to see if the fawn was still there.

"It's gone," he told me. I was glad to know that the mother had come and taken her baby to a safer place, away from the prying eyes of curious children.

As the day passed, I pondered over the events of the morning. Thinking about the large, black rat snake, I became unnerved. It was unsettling to think that such horrible creatures could live by the stream where our children liked to play. And the memory of that huge black serpent blocking the path to the church doors made me realize how real and sinister was the work of the devil. I began to feel scared and helpless, like the little fawn. And then Our Lady's message dawned on me: *Its mother is nearby . . . The mother will take care of her . . . The mother is definitely nearby and watching.*

Our Blessed Mother! Our unseen Mother! She is always nearby and watching. Weak and helpless though we are, she is ever ready to protect us! I remembered the words Our Lady spoke to St. Juan Diego:

> Do not fear any illness or vexation, anxiety or pain. Am I not here who am your Mother? Are you not under my shadow and protection? Am I not your fountain of life? Are you not in the folds of my mantle? In the crossing of my arms?[18]

---

18. Br. Michael, M.I.C.M., *Our Lady of Guadalupe*, catholicism.org, June 10, 2004, *http://catholicism.org/brmichael-guadalupe.html*.

Such consolation brought joy to my heart. With our Blessed Mother watching over us, we have no need to fear the schemes and machinations of the devil.

But we do need to be aware of them. If you go to Mass by yourself, he may likely throw obstacles in your way. However, if you bring your children with you, he will most certainly make it difficult, especially when your resolution is new and you are trying to establish a new routine. The devil knows that if you persevere in bringing your children to weekday Mass, your children will be lost to him. Their feet will be firmly planted on the path to sanctity and, furthermore, they will probably bring others to Christ, inspiring and evangelizing others without even knowing it, as only children can do.

Sometimes the devil is quite obvious, but more often, his tactics are subtle. The prince of lies wants to disguise his temptations and obstacles as "reasonable" excuses to skip weekday Mass or to miss your appointed time of prayer.

"You slept poorly last night," he likes to tell me. "It's okay if you sleep in. You need to get enough rest to keep up with your kids. You know how hard it is to be cheerful when you're exhausted." And what he says is true. But it's only half of the truth! And half-truths are even more deceiving than full-out lies because we see the kernel of truth and fall for the half-lie. The whole truth, in this case, is "Yes, you are tired and could use more rest. But how pleased our Lord will be if you make this sacrifice for him. What a torrent of graces he will pour out on you and your children because of this act of love. God will give you all the energy you need to fulfill his will today. Trust in him."

Our guardian angels can help us overcome any temptations and obstacles and make the way easier for us.

They wait for our invocations with great eagerness and will quickly come to our aid when we call for help. The Blessed Mother, whose very name will send the devil fleeing, is also ever-ready to help us in our efforts to come before her beloved son in the Holy Eucharist. Let us seek her protection and her intercession in obtaining for us the grace to persevere in our devotions to the Holy Eucharist.

"I am not called to be successful," wrote St. Teresa of Calcutta. "I am called to be faithful."[19] You may not succeed in getting to Mass every day, or as often as your state in life permits. You may not succeed in going to Adoration or visiting the Blessed Sacrament as often as you had resolved. In a busy, noisy household, you may not even succeed in spending fifteen or twenty minutes in quiet prayer with our Lord (at least, not without being distracted by your children or falling asleep from exhaustion). Thank God that he does not require us to be successful! The important thing is to be faithful. Keep on trying to spend time with our Lord in prayer. Never give up on your efforts to be united with him in Holy Communion. Persevere in enkindling in your hearts and the hearts of your children a burning, ardent love for Jesus in the Eucharist. Your faithfulness will bear much fruit, here on earth and in heaven. And the graces you obtain for your children will be the greatest gift, the most important treasure, by far, that you will and can ever impart.

---

19. Ray Cummings, *Are You Following Jesus?* (Xulon Press, 2003), p. 50.

4.

Evangelizing our Children with Joy

"Joy is a net of love by which we catch souls."
— SAINT TERESA OF CALCUTTA [1]

When I was a child, an advertisement came on frequently during one of my favorite TV shows. The advertisement was for a zoo, famous for its aquatic shows. It had a perky, catchy little tune, and there were clips of laughing children, smiling parents, and dancing dolphins. The song always ended with the words "Happiness is Marine Land." I saw this so many times, and the message became so engrained in my mind, that I began to believe it. I *had* to go to Marine Land to be happy, and I was so convinced that I was able to persuade my parents to take us there.

We saw the dolphin show. We looked at all the other animals. We ate hot dogs and ice cream. It was a lovely family outing. And yet, when I returned home, I had a rather unsettling feeling because I realized that happiness

---

1. Susan Conroy, *Mother Teresa's Lessons of Love & Secrets of Sanctity*, (Huntington, Ind.: Our Sunday Visitor Publishing, 2003), p. 20.

was *not* Marine Land. I wasn't any happier for having gone. I had expected that Marine Land would elevate me to a new level of happiness, and it did not. I had been duped by that advertisement with the laughing children and the perky little tune.

All children, like all other people, search for happiness. The quest for happiness is part of our longing for God, who alone can fulfill us. But, like any of us, children tend to search for happiness in fun, novelty, and pleasure. We need to show them where true happiness lies, which is in union with God. The closer we are to God and the more we unite our will with his, the happier we are.

St. Margaret Mary Alacoque wrote:

> It seems to me that the happiness of a soul consists entirely in conforming to the most adorable Will of God; for in so doing the heart finds peace and the spirit joy and repose.[2]

But how do we teach such an abstract concept in a concrete manner that children will understand? How do we prove to our children that true and lasting happiness is found not in toys, candies, novelties, and fun, but rather only in union with God? We prove it by our *joy*, the joy that comes from living the Gospel.

Children, by their very nature, are joyful, and they are very attracted to joy. The best way to evangelize our children is to be joyful, cheerful, and lighthearted. You can bring them to church all you want, send them to religious

---

2. Excerpt from a letter to Mother Louise de Soundeilles at Moulins from the monastery in Paray, January 6, 1683. *Blessed Letters of Saint Margaret Mary Alacoque*, *http://www.saintsbooks.net/books/St.%20Margaret%20Mary%20Alacoque%20-%20Letters.pdf*.

education classes, teach them the catechism, and pray with them daily, but unless they see, by your life and example, that the Gospel is indeed Good News and *tidings of great joy*, it will be hard to convince them that faith is the key to happiness.

"From somber devotions and sour-faced saints, good Lord, deliver us!" prayed St. Teresa of Avila.[3] Here is a saint who suffered much: poverty, sickness, painful migraines, constant obstacles, difficult people placed in her way, and forty years of spiritual dryness! It would have been easy for her to be sour-faced. And yet she is known for her cheerfulness, her sense of humor, and her contagious laughter. By her joy, she attracted many young women to her order and to a life that they knew would be filled with poverty, discomfort, and hardship. How attractive joy is!

As mothers, we too can suffer much: complicated pregnancies, colicky babies, sleepless nights, sick children, our own health problems, difficult teenagers, financial stresses, and so on. On any given day, there can be half-a-dozen problems that could cause us to feel moody, grumpy, annoyed, irritated, frustrated, or depressed.

And yet we are called to evangelize our children with joy. Joy! Being joyful doesn't mean that we have to be giddy or that we have to feel happy all the time. For joy is not simply an emotion. Joy is a state of being which transcends sufferings, trials, and worries and manifests itself in cheerfulness and lightheartedness.

Our children, who are often very tuned in to our emotions, need us to be joyful. And while joy itself is not an

---

3. James Martin, *Between Heaven and Mirth: Why Joy, Humor, and Laughter are at the Heart of the Spiritual Life*, (HarperOne; 4th Print edition), p.69.

emotion, it does keep our negative emotions in check. It helps us to control our feelings of anger, sadness, irritation, and impatience. As long as we are sad or angry, our children can never feel completely at ease. They are anxious and uncomfortable. In the back of our minds, we know this; perhaps that is why, when we are upset or moody, we often feel like bad mothers. We feel inadequate and discouraged. We must learn to overcome such emotions and beg God for the grace to be cheerful.

As our children get older, if we constantly give in to our negative emotions, they will notice the disconnect between what we profess to be our faith and how we actually live it. When children approach their teenage years, they become increasingly critical, not only of themselves but also of their parents. They will see, with increasing acuteness, our own weaknesses and faults. Does that mean we have to be perfect by the time our oldest turns twelve? Heaven forbid! But it does mean that we have to struggle heroically against our faults. We have to put a continuous effort into being cheerful, and we have to cultivate joy and kindness in our hearts. Then our children will see the unity in our lives, the beautiful cohesiveness between our faith and our everyday lives. They will see our joy in spite of our tribulations. And they will know, by our example and through the grace of God, where to look for true and lasting happiness.

So how do we arrive at this state of being—joy— which is so essential in evangelizing our children? Joy is one of the twelve fruits of the Holy Spirit. The others are patience, gentleness, self-control, charity, peace, kindness, goodness, generosity, modesty, faithfulness, and chastity. The Church describes these virtues as fruits because they are good habits that must be cultivated by constant practice and by God's grace. It seems to me that if joy is a fruit, then the tree that bears this fruit is our relationship with the Holy Spirit. The stronger and healthier our relationship with the Holy Spirit, the more fruit he will bear in our souls and in our character. And the basis of our relationship with the Holy Spirit, the roots of this tree, I believe, are a clear conscience, gratitude, and trust.

Joy begins with having a clear conscience, because then we are at peace with God. St. John Bosco said, "The young person who feels he is in a state of grace with God naturally experiences joy in the certainty that he possesses a good that is completely within his reach."[4] Similarly, St. Philip Neri expressed that "Christian joy is a gift from God, flowing from a good conscience."[5]

We all know the burden of guilt, the prick of the conscience when we have sinned, and the loss of peace that results from it. When guilt robs our soul of peace, our joy quickly dissipates. And so we need to avoid near occasions of sin and fight hard so as not to give into temptations. We want to avoid sin first and foremost because sin offends God, our Father, who is worthy of all our love. But we also try to avoid sin because sin weakens the will, clouds the intellect, and dampens our joy. When we fall, we should immediately appeal to the mercy of God. Going to confession on a frequent and regular basis will help keep our consciences free from guilt and restore peace to our souls.

---

4. John Bosco, *Vita del Giovanetto Savio Domenico*, in Opere Edite, XI, p. 236. Quoted in *The Four Pillars of Salesian Spirituality*, an article by Archbishop Angelo Amato, SDB, found on *http://www.ewtn.com/library/SPIRIT/SALESPIR.HTM*.

5. Martin, p. 77.

If we want to be joyful, we also need to develop a spirit of gratitude. Each day brings a shower of blessings and graces for which we ought to thank God: our children, husbands, and families, our homes and health, food on the table, a beautiful sunrise, a song that touches our hearts, a comforting phone call from a friend, the warm sun shining through the window and brightening up the room, and so on. So often we take these blessings for granted, and caught up in the busy-ness of life, we don't even notice them as being gifts of love from God. Moreover, the devil is always tempting us to sin against gratitude: to be pessimistic, to wallow in self-pity, to be envious, or to be preoccupied with what we don't have and what we need to get next. Just think how much time is wasted searching the internet for things we want but don't need!

Imagine a child on Christmas morning. After opening half a dozen presents that were carefully and lovingly prepared by her parents, she looks around, pushes her presents aside, and demands, "Are there any more?" How downcast her poor parents feel because of her ingratitude! And this is how we treat our Lord when we fail to thank him each day for his blessings.

One morning, I came down to the kitchen and saw that our Lord had painted a magnificent sunrise. Pink and purple clouds sailed high in the sky, through which the morning sun cast golden rays. The sheer beauty and peacefulness should have drawn me into a moment of wonder and contemplation, of thankfulness for this beautiful start to the day. But then I looked down and saw an irritating pile of dirty dishes in the sink. How easy it is to forget God's marvelous gifts!

When we are blinded by worldly distractions and our own greed or pride, we should pray like the beggar in the Gospel: "Lord, let me see again."[6] *Lord, grant that I may see all the good gifts you bring to me each day. May I be keenly aware of them so I can thank you again and again for your providence, your generous abundance of graces, and your love. Lord, grant me a heart full of gratitude.* Having a grateful heart opens wide the door to trust. If we are purposely mindful of all the good that God has done in our lives, if we can see his loving hand in every moment of each day, it becomes much easier to trust in his will, even when difficulties and sufferings arise. How our Lord longs for us to trust in him! And he does not want us to trust in him for his sake. Rather, he knows that it is only when we trust in him that we can be peaceful and joyful. It is only when we place all our concerns and worries into his hands and allow him to take charge that we can have the serenity of heart and peace of mind which allows us to be joyful.

If there is one thing all mothers are good at, it is worrying. Even before our babies are born, we worry. We worry about having a healthy baby and a safe delivery. After the baby is born, we worry about how much milk the baby is getting and how much weight the baby is gaining. We worry about allergies and sickness, we worry about how our children are faring in school, and we worry about whether or not they are making good friends. We worry about finances and how we will pay for their education. We worry about their future spouses, and we worry about the state of their souls. We worry about politics. We worry,

---

6. Lk 18:41.

and we worry, and then we worry about worrying. And all this worrying can make us stressed, overwhelmed, downhearted, and heavy.

How difficult it is to be joyful when we are bogged down by worry! When we are consumed by it, we need to recall all the good God has done in our lives and the countless times he has provided for our needs. Calling to mind specific examples of his love and mercy, of prayers answered, we say with grateful hearts, "Jesus, I trust in you!" This short prayer ought to be our mantra. For every worry that pops into our minds, we should immediately answer, "Jesus, I trust in you!" If you are like me, prone to constant worrying, what a blessing it will be! For all day long, you will be saying those words which are so sweet to our Lord: "Jesus, I trust in you!" Then your worries will lead you to prayer, and prayer will lead you to peace.

To further illustrate, consider our children, especially the really young ones who have not yet reached their teenage years. Children from loving and stable homes tend to be lighthearted and carefree. Why? Because they have so few worries. They don't worry about who will pay the bills or where the next meal will come from. They don't worry about catching a cold or getting cavities. They don't worry because they trust that their needs will be taken care of by their parents. And when they are naughty, they still don't worry because they know their parents will forgive them. And so they begin most days eager and optimistic, carefree and lighthearted.

Some of my fondest memories will always be seeing my children playing happily together without a care in the world. Children's bright smiles, the bounce in their steps, and their exuberant laughter give evidence of their simple trust in our love, our care, and our mercy. And yet we are but human, weak and sinful creatures who often make mistakes. If our children can be so joyful and trusting with such imperfect parents, how much more ought we to be joyfully trusting in God, who is perfect love and mercy, who never makes mistakes, and whose divine plan is for our eternal salvation and happiness?

So we see that a clear conscience, gratitude, and trust are the necessary conditions for joy, deep spiritual joy. Spiritual joy is an interior disposition. The external manifestation of joy is cheerfulness. Even when we are suffering, we can strive to be cheerful. And this is not "faking" happiness or playing the part of a clown, masking our misery with an artificial smile. Even in suffering, we can strive to be genuinely cheerful out of charity for others and because we trust that our sufferings, which are part of God's loving plan, will ultimately lead us to heaven.

One of the best things we can do for our children is to practice the virtue of cheerfulness. As I mentioned earlier, our children's emotions are very much tied to our own, and so they cannot feel truly happy if we are not happy. Our children thrive when they see our smiles and looks of approval or love, hear our laughter and words of praise, and feel our warm embraces or tickling fingers. And yet, you and I know what a huge sacrifice it can be at times just to smile, especially when we are tired and our patience has worn thin.

Spiritual joy is that deep gratitude and trust that gives peace to the soul. Cheerfulness means letting that joy shine through, even when our bodies and our emotions tell us that we are tired and out of sorts. Like all virtues, cheerfulness requires heroic practice. However, just as one muscle exercises another, the practice of cheerfulness helps us to grow in other virtues, especially those fruits of the Holy Spirit: self-control, peace, generosity, patience, and especially kindness.

How do we practice cheerfulness? We try to be patient when we're late for church and the toddler insists on putting on her own coat (which takes forever!). We smile at people even if we have a splitting headache. We try to be serene even when we are drowning in laundry and housework. Cheerfulness means we are good-humored even though we feel irritated by the constant nagging and bickering of our children. When our son knocks over a glass of milk for the umpteenth time, instead of angrily scolding, we kindly help him clean it up. And we try to deal with our children's annoying habits, immaturity, and carelessness with understanding, patience, and a sense of humor. One of the best practices of cheerfulness is to greet your husband lovingly and with a smile when he comes home from work, even if he is late *again*, and the kids have been driving you crazy all day.

Cheerfulness means we sing, laugh, dance, and play with our children, and not only when we feel like it but as often as we can. After all, we ought to sing and dance for joy because God loves infinitely and pours his graces upon us in abundance. And because we have abandoned our anxieties and worries into God's loving care, we should strive to be lighthearted. "Angels can fly," writes the witty Chesterton, "because they take themselves lightly."[7] With complete trust in God, our spirits can soar, too. "For my yoke is easy, and my burden is light."[8]

---

7. Chesterton, G.K. *Orthodoxy*, (Ortho Publishing, 2014), p. 121.
8. Mt 11:30.

We shouldn't take ourselves, our work, or even our mistakes too seriously. When the English martyr St. Thomas More was ascending the scaffolds for beheading, he jokingly said, "I pray you, I pray you, Mr. Lieutenant, see me safe up and for my coming down, I can shift for myself."[9] The third century martyr St. Lawrence was grilled to death over hot coals. As he lay burning, he called out to the executioners and quipped, "This side is done. Turn me over and have a bite!"[10] Even in death, these saints took themselves lightly. Let us imitate them when we feel as though we are being martyred. All those little things that bother and worry us should lead us to pray, "Jesus, I trust in you! It's your problem, not mine!" And then relax. God is in control.

We also ought to cultivate a sense of humor. Avoid that biting, sarcastic sense of humor that is so often hurtful. And refrain from cracking jokes at another's expense. Many couples do this to one another, and this causes unnecessary tension and hurt. Rather, nurture an appreciation for that which is wholesomely funny and amusing. I once knew a seminarian who, knowing his own tendency to be overly serious, made it a "serious" business to develop his sense of humor. He collected jokes and puns, wrote them in a notebook, and memorized them. His conversations were so peppered with jokes that he often kept us laughing. And he was so natural at it that we never guessed he put so much effort into being funny.

Blessed Francis Xavier Seelos, the Redemptorist priest who lived during the Civil War, had a wonderful sense of humor. One of his contemporaries wrote:

9. *https://en.wikipedia.org/wiki/Thomas_More#Trial_and_execution.*
10. Martin, p. 72.

Besides his piety and his profound erudition, he had an abundance of jokes and liked to tell them. When he told a joke, he would look at the person to whom he was telling it and laugh with such cordiality and hilarity that he was like a boy.[11]

In fact, Blessed Seelos enjoyed jokes so much that he formed a joke club with his seminarians. The rule of the club was that each seminarian was to tell a joke. If the joke was funny, they would all laugh. But if the joke was not, they were supposed to grunt. Seelos, however, laughed so hard and infectiously at all of the jokes that he was booted out of one of the meetings.[12]

Just as we ought to pray for and develop an awareness of all the gifts and graces God brings us, we can also learn to appreciate all the humorous things that happen each day. Young children, especially, are very cute and amusing, oftentimes without even trying to be so. We ought to savor and cherish their little antics and funny expressions, which are truly endearing. Even more, we should sometimes join in their silliness. I know that when we play silly games with our children, we often end up with a pack of unruly, rambunctious kids who laugh uncontrollably. However, the wonderful memories of joy we create far outlast the chaos.

St. Philip Neri, often known as the humorous saint, was often silly himself. Once he shaved off half his beard (only half!) before going to a ceremony given in his honor. Another time, in the middle of the summer, he wore a cushion on his head and a foxtail coat. These public acts of childish absurdity were his way of growing in humility. I

---

11. *http://www.seelos.org/2013_04_seelos_newsletter.pdf.*

12. *Seelos, Tireless Intercessor*, dir. John B. Clote, (Ignatius Press Studio, 2013).

also think it was a way to bring joy and laughter to others. Laughter was so important to him that he put a sign over his door that read *The House of Christian Mirth*.[13]

How children love such jokes! Our family is blessed to know a modern St. Philip Neri. Every time my children see this priest, they flock around him and the fun begins. He pretends to be a ninja, plays magical tricks, cracks jokes, and tells funny stories. He is a living example of the power and attractiveness of humor. And he is a reminder that we can and should use humor at home. For it can help divert impending tantrums and meltdowns, make scraped knees and black eyes feel better, and draw moody teenagers out of themselves. Wouldn't it be wonderful if our homes were also houses of Christian mirth, homes filled with laughter and joy?

Finally, we should learn to laugh at ourselves, for that will help us to become more humble and lovable. St. John XXIII also had a great sense of humor and a quick wit. Soon after being elected Pope, St. John XXIII was walking through the streets of Rome. A woman passed him, and realizing he was the new pope, exclaimed to her friend, "My God! He's so fat!" At that, St. John XXIII turned to her and replied, "Madame, I trust you understand that the papal conclave is not exactly a beauty contest."[14] He often joked about his round figure and plain appearance. Once, after a photography session, he looked up at the tall, elegant Archbishop Fulton Sheen and joked, "From all eternity, God knew that I was going to be pope. He had eighty years to work on me. Why did he make me so ugly?" Another time, with the pretense of a sigh, he said

---

13. Martin, p. 77.
14. Martin, p. 79.

to a visitor who had a lean physique, "We will both have to say a prayer to God, beseeching him to remove half my excess fat to give it to you."[15] Like St. Philip Neri, St. John XXIII used humor as a way to grow in humility and spread a little joy.

Cheerfulness, the exterior manifestation of spiritual joy, is a virtue that is highly prized by the saints because it attracts others to the faith.

St. Teresa of Calcutta encouraged her sisters to be cheerful:

> Cheerfulness is a sign of a generous person. It is often a cloak that hides a life of sacrifice. A person who has this gift of cheerfulness often reaches great heights of perfection . . . Joy is very infectious; therefore, be always full of joy when you go among the poor.[16]

St. Josemaría Escrivá wrote about cheerfulness in *Furrow*:

> The cheerfulness of a man of God, a woman of God has to overflow: it has to be calm, contagious, attractive . . . in short, it has to be so supernatural and natural, so infectious, that it brings others to follow the Christian way.[17]

And St. Padre Pio taught: "Joy, with peace, is the sister of charity. Serve the Lord with laughter."[18]

---

15. Louise Perrotta, "Two Saints Who Smiled," *The Word Among Us*, Nov. 2013, https://wau.org/archives/article/two_saints_who_smiled.

16. Mother Teresa, *Love: a Fruit Always in Season: Daily Meditations from the Words of Mother Teresa of Calcutta*, ed. Dorothy S. Hunt, (Ignatius, 1987), p. 109.

17. St. Josemaría Escrivá, *Furrow*, (Scepter, 2011), 60.

18. Bernard Ruffin, *Padre Pio: The True Story*, (Huntington, Ind.: Our Sunday Visitor, 1991), p. 144.

If we want to draw our children to the faith, we must work at being very cheerful. Of course, this is not easy. But cheerfulness, when it is an outpouring of a deep spiritual joy, and with constant effort and practice, will become habitual and natural. How true is the saying, "If Mama ain't happy, ain't nobody happy!" When we are cheerful, our children often reflect this cheerfulness back. With cheerfulness, we become witnesses of God's love to our families. And in turn, our families become witnesses of the joy of the Gospel to the world.

5.

Kindness

THE SISTER OF JOY

"Be the living expression of God's kindness—kindness in your face, kindness in your eyes, kindness in your smile, kindness in your warm greeting."

— SAINT TERESA OF CALCUTTA[1]

In the last chapter, we saw that joy stems from a peaceful conscience, gratitude for God's blessings, and deep trust in our Lord. There is one final ingredient, which our Lord makes very clear: when his joy is in us, our joy is complete. And his joy is in us when we keep his Great Commandment, "Love one another as I have loved you."[2]

As the Father has loved me, so have I loved you; abide in my love. If you keep my commandments, you will abide in my love, just as I have kept my Father's commandments and abide in his love. These things I have spoken to you, that my joy may be in you, and that your

---

1. Susan Conroy, *Mother Teresa's Lessons of Love & Secrets of Sanctity*, (Huntington, Ind.: Our Sunday Visitor, 2003), p. 64.

2. Jn 15:12.

joy may be full. This is my commandment, that you love one another as I have loved you.[3]

If we want to keep Christ's command to love each other as he has loved us, we need to imitate his love. Our love has to be a love that causes us to die to self. Our love has to be selfless and sacrificial. Just as joy is made manifest with genuine cheerfulness, love is made manifest with acts of kindness. And sacrificial love, Christ-like love, is made manifest with sacrificial acts of kindness.

Kindness. It sounds so simple, doesn't it? And yet, at times it requires much effort. Have you noticed that it is often easier to be kind to friends, colleagues, and even strangers than it is to be kind to the ones whom we love the most—our husbands and children? I suppose it is because we let our guards down when we are with our own families. We are not afraid to show our moodiness, sarcasm, or temper. Moreover, our children, with their bickering and nagging, their whining and carelessness, their disobedience and disrespect, can drive us to insanity. And then, because our children are ours, we do not see them with the same objectivity and detachment as we view other children. Our expectations are sometimes unrealistic, and so we become frustrated with them. In our frustration, we sometimes spout out unkind words. Indeed, it can be very hard to be kind to our children when they test our patience and our self-control to their limits and beyond.

And yet, kindness is a necessary ingredient in evangelizing our children. For it is through kindness that we win their hearts, their confidence, and their trust. Furthermore,

3. Jn 15:9–12.

it is almost impossible to be cheerful when one has been uncharitable. When we give in to anger and frustration and say mean words or inflict a punishment that we know is unjust or too harsh, our moods plunge into discouragement and deeper frustration. The reason for this is that one of the conditions for joy is to have a clear conscience. When we have been unkind, our consciences prick us and our guilt makes it impossible to feel at peace. We know we have hurt our children, whom we love so much, and this hurts us even more. Sadness and guilt set in as we realize that we have been pathetic witnesses of God's love and mercy.

Thankfully, God is forgiving and our children are, too. But for every unkind word or deed, we need to apologize and ask for our children's forgiveness. Yes, this means we eat humble pie. But humble pie is a very good antidote to pride and selfishness, which are usually the deepest roots of sin.

For example, suppose you are trying to help your son memorize the multiplication tables. He has already put up a big stink about having to work on the multiplication tables because he would rather be playing outside. But you are calm, and you try to motivate him. Cheerfully, you offer to make a game of it. Your surly son grumbles but goes along with the game. However, he becomes increasingly unsettled as it becomes apparent that he is still really struggling to recall the facts.

"Aww, can we stop now? We've done enough!" he pleads.

"No, you really need to master at least the six times tables," you answer. And in the back of your mind you are thinking, "Why can't he get these facts? We've been practicing them for two months now!" Meanwhile, your pride is suggesting, "This is *my* son! He should know these by now! Surely he's as smart as everyone else in his class, if not smarter! He ought to be at the top of his class!"

Maybe your son was lazy and irresponsible and did not study as well as he should have. Or maybe, truly and objectively, your son did put in a good effort but just needs more time, help, and encouragement. But pride clouds your judgment, as happens with everyone, and you begin to think that he is just plain lazy.

After a few more incorrect guesses, your son asks, more emphatically, "Can we stop now? We've been doing this foreverrrrr!"

"No!" you say, with an edge in your voice. "I told you that you need to memorize the six times tables. Now!" Eventually, his and your frustration mount, and you break out into a yelling match with your son. Angry words of ridicule fly from your mouth. As your crying son gets up and rushes to his room, you yell out, "And you can stay there until you have them memorized!"

Pride, wretched pride, lies at the root of misunderstanding, frustration, and anger. Pride lies at the root of misery. When we have lost our tempers with our children and hurt their feelings with our unkind words or over-reactive and unjust punishments, we need to humbly ask for forgiveness. The more we have hurt them, the more humble our contrition should be, even if it means kneeling before them and taking them into our arms as we acknowledge our fault. In this way, we grow in humility and assuage any hurt or resentful feelings our children may have. Do not leave your children to stew in resentment, as this often leads to rebellion or passive-aggressive behavior. You must make amends with your children and reassure them that you love them. Do not take it for granted that your child knows he is loved and feels loved. Children need to be told and shown again and again that they are loved deeply and unconditionally, especially when they have been hurt.

We also need to seek God's pardon whenever we have been unkind to our children. After all, they are his children—entrusted to our care, of course, but his beloved children. Saying a prayer of contrition and resolving to do better mark a good starting place, but the best way to root out pride and any weakness such as impatience or a quick temper is to go to frequent and regular confession. How frequent? "At least once a month," according to St. John Bosco.[4] Every time we go to confession, not only are we forgiven our sins, but we also grow in humility and receive graces that help us not to repeat the same sins again.

The spiritual effects of the sacrament of Penance are:

- reconciliation with God by which the penitent recovers grace;
- reconciliation with the Church;
- remission of the eternal punishment incurred by mortal sins;
- remission, at least in part, of temporal punishments resulting from sin;
- peace and serenity of conscience, and spiritual consolation;
- an increase in strength for the Christian battle.[5]

---

4. *http://saintbosco.org/quotes/index.php?cat=17.*

5. CCC, 1496

Many men and women have rid their souls of deeply rooted sinful habits by the graces obtained through frequent and regular confession. So, if you want to overcome your impatience, your quick temper, or the pride that causes you to be unkind to your children, persevere in going to confession often.

St. Ignatius of Loyola taught the Jesuits a spiritual practice that can be very helpful to mothers, especially in our efforts to be kind and patient. This practice is called *agere contra*, which is Latin for "to act against." It refers to our acting against temptations, against our sinful tendencies, and against our natural inclinations when they could lead us into sin.

We all face temptations, and we all have sinful tendencies. It is generally clear that we need to work against them. We fight laziness by working hard. We fight pride with acts of docility and humility. We try to control our quick tempers by holding our tongues when angry. But what about our natural inclinations? What about those tendencies which are usually construed as virtuous but sometimes lead to sin?

For example, it is a virtue to be tidy and orderly. But if we find ourselves yelling at our kids every time they trek mud into the house, we need to act against our compulsion to keep a clean floor, at least until we can calmly and charitably get our kids to clean up the mess. It is better to tolerate a messy floor with charity than to have a spotless house but a sullied soul.

Tendencies that seem virtuous can become excessive, usually when the motivations behind them are disordered. I love a sparkling clean house. When the house is clean, I feel happy and peaceful. However, I need to act against my desire for perfect neatness or I will drive my children crazy with constant nagging. If I insisted on the kids keeping the house spotless all day long, I would be acting selfishly. After all, I am not the only one living in our home. When we have guests over, of course we want our homes to be clean and inviting. It is a sign of welcome and respect. But if pride creeps in and becomes the main motivation for cleaning the house, we would do well to practice *agere contra* and leave a little mess in order to grow in humility.

Agere contra can help us find the healthy medium between being the fun-loving Disney Mom or the strict Tiger Mom. Many of us tend to lean one way or the other. Are you a fun-loving, easygoing mother? Wonderful! Your children will probably have many happy memories of fun times and family adventures. But use *agere contra* to prevent yourself from neglecting your responsibilities in your desire for fun and excitement. Being easygoing is generally a virtue and can signify great trust in God. But it can deteriorate into laziness, procrastination, or a lack of consistency and routine that many children need in order to thrive.

Are you a strict, disciplinary mother? Great! Your children will learn to work hard, and with the self-discipline you teach them, they will probably become accomplished, well-educated adults. But use *agere contra* to avoid the trap of becoming too ambitious, too rigid in your schedule, or too authoritative in your approach. Being disciplined is a virtue and a sign of interior strength. But it can deteriorate into insensitivity and impatience toward others, and a lack of the warmth and spontaneity that children so love.

Whether you are a Disney Mom, a Tiger Mom, or someone in-between, you can practice *agere contra* by praying for the wisdom to understand the motivations behind your actions and decisions. Whenever you see that your driving motivation is not charity, but rather pride, selfishness, fear, laziness, or anything else that is not of God, then act against it by doing the opposite of what you are inclined to do.

Practicing *agere contra* helps us to grow in kindness in many ways. First, it moderates any tendencies we have that would otherwise become excessive or compulsive. Second, the practice of *agere contra* requires us to pray. Without the wisdom and insights of the Holy Spirit, we will not be able to discern the true motivations behind our inclinations. The action of prayer itself draws us closer to Christ and makes us more like Him—and therefore more charitable. Third, the practice of going against our inclinations teaches us to die to self for the sake of others. It makes our hearts more disposed to sacrificial kindness and generosity. Finally, the more we die to self, the more we learn not to insist on our own wills but to embrace the will of God, which is always the most loving and charitable path.

Kindness is not just the avoidance of unpleasant or hurtful behavior towards others. It is the habit of being considerate, thoughtful, and generous toward others in word and deed. Like cheerfulness, kindness is a very attractive virtue that wins the hearts of others. As flowers turn toward the sun, so do children naturally gravitate toward those who treat them with kindness.

Kindness toward our children begins with this fundamental fact: They are God's children, made in his image and likeness, and are thus worthy of respect and dignity. Although they don't always act like children of God, they are still his children and we ought to treat them as such.

Being kind to our children means we patiently help them when they need help. We listen to their prattle with full attention. We read to them and play with them. We show our children that we enjoy their company. Once in a while, we cook their favorite meals, just as a treat. We take them out on dates. We praise and encourage them. We greet them warmly. We tuck them in at bedtime and bless them. There are countless opportunities each day to be kind to our children, and all they really require is for us to take the time to make each act of kindness.

And yet that's the hard part: taking the time, or rather, giving it. As mothers, we can be so busy, so very busy, taking care of our families and homes that we easily brush our children aside. We get impatient when they require a lot of our time to help them with their schoolwork or other projects. When our children try to talk to us, we don't always listen carefully; perhaps we are too busy browsing the internet or texting. We cannot seem to find the time to read to them, and when they ask us to play with them, we say, "Maybe later on," but often, 'later on' fails to happen. In our haste to complete our never-ending to-do lists, it is hard to take time out of our hectic days to make little acts of kindness.

If the care of your busy household and an overwhelming amount of work is making it very difficult for you to stop what you are doing and take the time to give your child a little loving attention, start saying the little prayer, "Jesus, I trust in You."

Jesus, I trust that you will give me the grace to do what really needs to be done and that you will take care of the rest. And then, as much as possible, stop multi-tasking and slow down. I know that when you have young children, that can be nearly impossible. It is hard to bake a batch of cookies without having to stop and take your toddler to the potty, pull your little climber off the table, or break up a sibling squabble. Interruptions to our work abound. But when our children interrupt our work because they need our help, we should give them our full attention. Do not hastily and impatiently hurry them along, but rather, with love and kindness, and with a cheerful smile, give them the help they need. In this moment, God is calling you through the voice of your child. Answer Him with love.

> Whoever receives one such child in my name receives me; and whoever receives me, receives not me but him who sent me."[6]

One year, a college roommate of mine, Maria, who was a medical student, went to India to work with Saint Teresa of Calcutta's Sisters of Charity. She was helping to distribute meals to a very long line of impoverished people. As she watched one of the sisters hand out the meals, Maria became impatient. The long line was moving ever so slowly as the sister and the other volunteers took their sweet time, chatting and smiling while leisurely doling out the food. Finally, Maria could bear it no longer. She turned to the sister and said, "Sister, we could get through this line much more quickly and efficiently. Just watch." Maria was about to start serving in an expedient assembly-line fashion, when the sister gently stopped her.

"Maria," she said kindly. "It's not about efficiency. It's about love."

---

6. Mk 9:37.

It's about love. How beautiful! The sisters knew they were not just feeding bodies. They were feeding souls with their smiles, their warm greetings, and their kind words. We too are not just feeding bodies and minds. We too are feeding souls, and nourishing our children's souls is one thing we cannot rush through. It is not something that can be done quickly or efficiently, and certainly not impatiently. The only way to tend to our children's souls is with love, kindness, understanding, and patience; and this takes time.

Instead of focusing on what we want to do each day, let's fix our thoughts on what we want to *be*: kind, loving, cheerful mothers. Let's make acquiring the virtue of kindness more important than completing our to-do lists. Every interruption and every setback can be an opportunity to actively practice kindness. Even more, we can seek and plan opportunities to express our love for our children, little acts of kindness with which we can win their trust, confidence, and love, so they will whole-heartedly follow us along the path to Christ.

6.

Understanding
THE WAY TO PATIENCE

Let your understanding strengthen your patience.
— ST. PETER DAMIEN[1]

One of the most common day-to-day challenges of parenting is being patient with our children. Children seem to be born with the propensity to test our patience. When do we become impatient with our children? When they dilly-dally, goof-off, or daydream during school or while doing homework. We become impatient when they are not learning a skill or understanding a concept as fast as we expect. Our patience is tested when we are trying to rush our children out the door for an appointment and they are lollygagging, oblivious that the clock is ticking. Sometimes we feel impatient when we repeatedly give them instructions that they ignore or forget: *Shut the door; turn off the lights; take off your shoes; make your bed; close the fridge; don't bite your nails!* Or how about when we're on the phone and our children start badgering us for a snack or some other request? Doesn't that test

---

1. Ronda Chervin, *Quotable Saints*, (Marian Publishers 2003), p. 22.

our patience? Often without even trying to, our precious children drive us batty by pushing our patience to the limit and beyond. Growing in patience requires us to exercise self-control, to subdue our tempers, and to work hard at being kind when we want to snap at one of our kids or yell. It means correcting our children with firmness yet kindness when they are careless, forgetful, or flat-out disobedient. But I think our patience grows most when we are understanding and thus have realistic expectations, and when we trust in God's perfect timing.

Our Children's Sense of Time

First, we need to understand our children's sense of time. Time moves much more slowly for children than for adults, and the younger a child is, the more slowly time seems to move. Conversely, as a person gets older, time seems to pass more quickly. An hour can seem like an eternity for a young child, whereas for most adults, an hour goes by very quickly. Ten minutes usually seems like a decent chunk of time for a child. So when you tell your young son that he has ten minutes to clean up, in his mind, that's enough time to build a fort, play a new game, *and* clean up. Of course, he is wrong, but he's still learning to manage his time. When ten minutes has passed and you see that he has only begun to clean up, the temptation is to accuse him of being a lazy procrastinator. And perhaps that is the case. But there is always the possibility that his slow sense of time made him lose track of absolute time. We ought to be understanding and try to help him develop a more accurate sense of time. I have found that setting a timer in a place where my children can see it helps to give them a sense of how much time they have to complete a task.

Because time moves much more slowly for our children than for us, they live at a slower pace. They do not and ought not live at the same fast, sometimes frenetic, pace of the adult world. From their perspective, time moves slowly. There is plenty of it, so why rush? Also, children do not have the same sense of purpose or consequence as their parents do. And so, they generally don't care about wasting time or being on time.

As parents, we need to teach our children to use their time well and to be responsible and punctual. But if we think that we are going to get our children up to an adult's level of time management and efficiency before they are teens, and in some cases, young adults, we set ourselves up for a lot of frustration. The kinder, more realistic and appropriate thing to do is to meet them somewhere in the middle. Patiently encourage your children to work in a timely, more responsible manner while slowing down your own clock and the pace of your life to be more in sync with theirs. Often this means simplifying your schedule. You can simplify your schedule by not cramming your child's day with too many structured activities. Children need time to lollygag, daydream, and live in imaginary worlds. They need time to pursue their own interests at their own pace. This is a beautiful part of childhood that we as parents can enjoy and savor as long as we respect our children's pace of life.

Temperament and Personality

The better we understand our children, the easier it is to be patient with them. We can become so preoccupied with planning, working, taking our children from one activity to another, and teaching them that we don't actually study them. Yes! We need to study our children, because that, along with prayer, is how we will understand them. By listening to our children, conversing with them, and observing them carefully, we can begin to understand our children's learning styles, their temperaments and personality traits, their love languages, and what motivates them. Try to figure out your child's learning style. Is he an auditory, visual, or a kinesthetic learner? What is his temperament? Extrovert or introvert? Is he choleric (strong-willed and driven), melancholic (idealistic, creative, perfectionistic and moody), sanguine (eager, sociable, fun-loving, and optimistic), or phlegmatic (co-operative, peaceful, and easy-going), or a combination? Is your child a perfectionist, or does he tend to be sloppy? Is he high-strung or mellow? Sensitive or tough? Chatty or monosyllabic? Focused or easily distracted? Serious or happy-go-lucky? Art and Lorraine Bennet have written a wonderful book, *The Temperament God Gave Your Kids*. It is worthy reading for parents who want to understand their children's personalities, natural virtues, and weaknesses more deeply. When you identify and understand your children's learning styles and temperaments, you will gain much wisdom and insight regarding your children's behavior, and how to teach, motivate, and discipline them.

The Love Languages

My husband and I particularly find Gary Chapman's *The Five Love Languages of Children* to be very helpful in dealing with our children. It is a mistake to assume that our children know and feel loved. We need to constantly affirm our children and let them know how deeply they are loved. But according to Chapman, when a child's love language is different from his parents', the parents need to pay extra attention to the child's love language—because people tend to express their love in the ways they want to be loved. People who love to receive gifts usually give gifts as a sign of love. People who highly value quality time will show love by trying to spend quality time with those whom they love. If we know what our children's love languages are, we can focus our efforts into expressing our love in their languages as opposed to our own.

The five love languages are: affection, words of affirmation, gifts, quality time, and acts of service. Most people prefer one or two over the others. For example, my daughter's love languages are gifts and words of affirmation. She treasures the gifts people give her, and words of encouragement are very dear to her because these make her feel loved. Hence, in my daily interactions with her, I need to encourage her very often. When I need to constructively criticize or correct her work, I begin by pointing out what she did well, then I move on to the corrections with extra sensitivity and with plenty of praise and encouragement. When she is struggling with a subject and feeling discouraged, I am often amazed at how a small gift, such as a piece of chocolate, will quickly perk her up.

My middle son, Joseph, thrives on acts of service. He shows his love by eagerly helping out around the house. However, he needs to be shown that he is loved through acts of service. A year ago, Joseph was having some issues with doing his math. I would give him a sheet with twenty math facts to complete, and he would insist that he couldn't do them; the work was too hard and he couldn't remember the facts. Joseph was adamant about needing help. I knew very well that he could do the work independently because he had done the same sheet daily for the past week. Each day he had insisted that he needed help. Yet, whenever I sat down with him and did just a few facts with him, Joseph was fine and completed the rest on his own. I realized that, as an acts-of-service person, Joseph needed my help not because he couldn't do the math but because he wanted to feel loved. I had made a mistake in pushing him to be independent when he wasn't emotionally ready for it. After a few weeks of "helping" Joseph with his math facts, he began to request my help less and less. Knowing his love language helped me to understand his behavior and to be patient with him.

Birth Order

Sometimes we have unrealistic expectations of our children, and this can cause frustration and impatience. This is particularly true with our firstborn children. Often, we expect our eldest children to excel in school and sports, to be responsible and mature, to help out around the house, and to take care of younger siblings. And very often they do, because children have a remarkable ability to meet expectations. But sometimes we raise the bar too high, causing our children a lot of stress and ourselves a lot of frustration. We are often impatient with our firstborns. We want them to behave like grown-ups too quickly. Perhaps it is because when we each have our first, we do not yet realize how quickly the years will pass. We fuss and fret over all the big milestones, such as toilet training and learning to read, as if it will take our children "forever" to learn these things. We give them toys that are too advanced and enroll them in activities they are not ready for. Take, for example, the two-year-old at the expensive amusement park who only wants to feed the ducks, or the four-year-old who sits in the outfield and picks grass during a T-ball game. The high expectations we have of our eldest children can be beneficial. Eldest children do tend to become high achievers and responsible adults. But when our expectations are too high, we place a lot of unnecessary strain on our children, ourselves, and on our relationships with them.

With subsequent children, our intensity begins to mellow as we gain wisdom and experience but lose a little energy and drive. Our expectations become more realistic but the opposite tendency can begin to creep in: expecting too little and even babying the youngest. In families with multiple children, there is a tendency to make the older siblings give in to the younger ones and to be more lenient and permissive with the younger children. The danger here is that the older children may resent this unfairness. This resentment often shows up in an older child's passive-aggressive behavior toward younger siblings. We need to ask ourselves: *Are the expectations I have for my younger children tempered by experience and wisdom? Or are they lowered because I am busier, worn down, and too tired to handle my kids with the same energy I had when I was younger and had fewer children?* We must continue to see each child's potential for greatness and sanctity and work toward it with the same fervor and passion as with our first. Otherwise, the younger ones may not aspire to the heights of excellence, virtue, and holiness of which they are capable.

Gender Differences

One area where we can go awry in expectations of our children is to expect our boys to behave like girls or vice-versa. Of course, each child is unique, but boys generally play and think differently from girls. Dr. Leonard Sax, a psychologist and pediatrician, gives compelling evidence for this in his book *Gender Matters*.[2]

We do our young boys a great disservice when we expect them to sit and study at their desks quietly and without being distracted. Boys need to stand, move, fidget, go outside, and blow off steam. They feel an irresistible urge to test the limits of their strength and endurance, again and again. And so they have a compulsion to contend with nature, build snow forts, stomp in puddles, dig into the ground, climb trees, and belly flop into the water. Boys like to compete in things they are good at because they want to know where they stand in the pecking order. And most boys love action, especially when it's exciting. Certainly, as they mature, boys will settle down and be able to concentrate and be still for longer periods of time. But when we teach boys, we need to be very understanding and patient, expecting and allowing for a certain amount of restlessness and movement.

A frequent challenge in teaching girls is dealing with their sensitivity and emotions. A friend of mine is in the reserves for the Canadian army. For several years, he taught at an all-boys school. The boys loved his military approach

---

2. Andrew Paduwa, founder of the Institute for Excellence in Writing, gives a wonderful overview of Dr. Sax's book in the first part of a talk entitled "Teaching Boys and Other Kids who Would Rather Build Forts." The second part of this excellent talk is about motivation and relevance. It is available for download at *www.iew.com*.

to teaching. My friend would yell out commands, and the boys would respond promptly and eagerly. After a few years, he started a new job teaching at a co-ed school. His military style of teaching, which had been a huge success at the boys' school, was not well received at the co-ed school. Several girls thought he was yelling at them. They took it personally and began to cry.

When I taught at an all-girls' high school, I learned that a girl's relationship with the teacher strongly affects her interest and sometimes even her ability to excel in whatever subject the teacher is teaching. While this is true for most children, boys and girls alike, it is especially so for girls. Most girls need to feel that the teacher likes them, cares for them, and wants them to succeed. If a girl feels that the teacher is coldly indifferent toward her, she is very likely to lose any motivation and interest she had for the subject. When our daughters are struggling with their studies, we need to look first at their relationship with their teachers and seek to reconcile any rifts or misunderstandings that may exist. Again, here is where understanding our children's love languages is helpful, because such understanding will show how best to speak to their hearts and help them feel loved. Only when they feel loved or well-liked by their teachers will most girls thrive in school.

Character Development

One trap that we sometimes fall into is that of being overly critical of our children. Sometimes we get too caught up in trying to correct our children's faults and bad habits that we forget any natural virtues they may have. When this happens, we often come across as being judgmental. Our children perceive the negative image that we have of them and sometimes become withdrawn and discouraged with trying to be good. Comparing our children's faults to the virtues or achievements of other children only exacerbates the problem. "Look how tidy Susie keeps her room. She is so neat and orderly. Your room is a disaster. Why can't you keep your room clean the way she does?" Such comments only cause hurt and discouragement. Rarely do they motivate. And often, they only make us feel more vexed and irritated as parents.

Again and again we must remind ourselves that our children are children of God. Yes, they are born with original sin, which becomes glaringly evident as they enter into toddlerhood. Nonetheless, they are intended for great holiness. Our children need to be convinced of this. They need to believe in their capacity for sanctity and heroism. So, we need to focus on our children's natural goodness; brainstorm and make a list, if you must. Each child has some natural virtues that he seems to be born with. My son can be a terror towards other boys, but he is remarkably tender and protective toward his little sister, and he has a magnanimous heart. My other son is highly explosive and reactive, but he gets over disputes and disappointments very quickly. He is quick to obey and careful with his work. My daughter is very sensitive and has difficulty accepting criticism, but she is extremely responsible, diligent, and sweet-tempered. *What are the good qualities of each of your children? What are their natural virtues?* When they exhibit these virtues, praise them lavishly and point them out to other family members. "Did you boys notice how well Henry made his bed this morning? Henry, you did such a great job! And I didn't even have to tell you to do it! I bet you could do a great job like that every day." If we do this frequently, we encourage our children to develop these virtues even more, we inspire siblings to imitate such goodness, and we nurture in our children positive self-identities.

As for their faults, we need to be aware of them and expect them. But more importantly, we need to have a plan for how we will help our children overcome their personal defects and weaknesses. Does your child have a bad temper? Help him find ways to control his anger. Does your child always seek immediate gratification? Make him wait, work toward, and earn the toys and treats he thinks he has to have right now. Delayed gratification often leads to increased appreciation. Does your child have a tendency to be selfish? Make him practice acts of charity: sharing, giving toys away, donating money to the poor, and serving others. Very often, a vice can be overcome by working hard to practice the opposite virtue, especially when accompanied by grace and prayer.

Having a plan for how you will help your child overcome his sinful habits or inclinations is of great value, for when your child makes a transgression, instead of it becoming a moment of annoyance and impatience for you, it becomes a teachable moment. Imagine that you are working at the computer and all of a sudden, you hear a shriek and then crying from another room. There is a patter of footsteps, and in bursts your son, bawling his eyes out. "Mommy! David hit me!" he wails. In stomps David.

"But Sam took my Lego piece and won't give it back!" he yells. How do we deal with the situation? If we have a plan for dealing with David's temper, we will likely be more patient, calm, and just in administering disciplinary action because we already know what we are going to do and we know that here is an opportunity to help him grow in virtue. If we don't have a plan, we are more likely to be frustrated, unjust, impatient, and reactionary. In our impatience to get back to our work, we may choose the quickest solution, but it may not be the fairest or best one. Of course, there is no possible way to have a plan for every upset, dispute, and transgression our children will present. But if we have a plan for the *habitual* ones, little by little and one at a time, we can help our children overcome their faults.

How do we come up with a plan for helping our children overcome their defects of character? How can we know if our expectations of our children are realistic and appropriate? We should read good books on parenting, seek the advice of trustworthy friends, study and observe our children, but above all, we need to pray, pray, pray. As we study our children to understand their learning styles, temperaments, natural virtues, and weaknesses, we need to bring these observations to our prayers. We need to pray to the Holy Spirit for guidance in planning how to help our children overcome their defects. We need to ask the Holy Spirit to increase our understanding and to show us what are *his* expectations and goals for each of our children, especially when we plan our children's curriculums, activities, chores, and schedules. We will save our children a lot of tears and stress, and ourselves a lot of frustration, if we are proactive in disciplining our children and if our expectations are a reflection of God's expectations.

Scheduling in Serenity

Very often it is easy to lose patience with our children when we are pressed for time. Do you ever feel like you never have enough hours in the day to do all that you think needs to be done? Do you often stay up late, depriving yourself of necessary sleep in order to get work done? Do you rush from one activity or commitment to the next? Do you ever have the guilty feeling that you are not spending enough quality time with your children? Do you feel as if you are too busy to pray? The feeling of having too much work and too little time can certainly make us feel impatient and stressed.

When the answer to some of the questions above is "yes," we need to consider the possibility that some of the activities we cram into our days are not God's will but our own. Perhaps you wake up each morning with a mental list of all the things you plan to do that day. Take this list to our Lord during your morning prayer and ask him if there is anything in that list that is not his will, and if there is anything missing from your list that he wants you to do. *Lord, what is your will for me today? Help me to be faithful in doing your will, not mine.* Some things are almost certain: our Lord wants us to spend time in prayer. He wants us to spend time teaching our children about the Faith, whether by word or example. He wants us to raise our children's hearts and minds to him. He wants us reflect his love with patience, kindness, joy, and forgiveness. And he wants us to trust in him. All other activities, such as sports, music lessons, birthday parties, and clubs, are things we need to pray about and discern.

If we strive to do *only* what God wills and if we trust that doing his will is "sufficient," our expectations of how we schedule our days will be much more realistic. We can overcome the urge to keep up with other families or enroll in too many activities. We will feel much less stressed, and it will be easier to be patient and kind with our children. Truly, in scheduling our days and our children's days, less is more, because unless we waste our time watching TV, playing video games, or surfing the internet, we will have more time for the most important things: spending quality time with our children, teaching them about the love of God, enjoying relaxed family dinners, and sitting at the feet of Christ in prayer.

When you are planning your schedule, expect accidents, meltdowns, sibling squabbling, and other small disasters and inconveniences. Schedule in buffer time to accommodate them because they are inevitable. The younger your children are, the more buffer time you need. If you have little ones and it takes you fifteen minutes to get out the door, plan for twenty-five minutes so you won't feel stressed when your toddler suddenly has to go potty or one of your children trips and skins his knee and you can't find the Band-Aids. If you think it will take your daughter forty-five minutes to complete her math, plan for an hour. If it so happens that you actually arrive at an event early, or your children actually finish their schoolwork faster than expected, rejoice! You can use that unused buffer time for extra prayer, a cup of tea, or playtime with your kids. Buffer time gives us breathing space and allows us to feel more serene. It is much easier to be patient and kind with our children when we feel that we are ahead of the game, or at least on time.

"Love is patient, love is kind . . ."[3]

As we strive to be patient and understanding toward our children, we must strive to be especially so with our husbands. The very best thing a mother can do for her children is to love their father. The very best thing a father can do for his children is to love their mother. When children grow up in a family rooted in a strong, loving marriage, they experience firsthand the unconditional, forgiving, and merciful love of God and a sense of security that will later help them to trust God in all things. The happiness of our children and our families depends especially on the happiness of our marriages. So we need to love our husbands, and love them faithfully, with patience, kindness, and understanding.

Our loves should be ordered in this way: God first, our husbands second, our children third, and other family members and friends fourth. Caught up in the consuming task of caring for our children, we can easily forget this order of love and put our love for our husbands on the back burner. Unless we constantly endeavor to renew our love for our husbands, to spend one-on-one time with them, to kindle the flames of romance, and to show our love with respect, patience, and kindness, our love will wane.

Love is a verb, an action, a choice, so much more than it is a noun, a feeling. During our wedding vows, we promised to love and honor our husbands all the days of our lives. To love and to honor—these are active verbs, *doing* verbs. Feelings of love and feelings of respect may come and go, but we must be constant and faithful in lov*ing* and

---

3. 1 Corinthians 13:4

honor*ing* our husbands regardless of our feelings, which at times can be so fickle.

When you first fell in love with your husband, it is possible that the "feeling" of love was so strong that it was easy to love. You loved because you felt love. I think God often does this in order to draw a couple together for marriage. After marriage, our love needs to mature. The action of love needs to come before the feeling of love. This is especially true when difficulties, frictions, and disagreements arise, and the feeling of love is temporarily lost. In the words of St. John of the Cross, "Where there is no love, put love, and there you will find love."[4]

The epitome of love is on the crucifix: Christ, tormented and ridiculed, dying on the cross for the sake of our souls. He teaches us that real love is shown when we make sacrifices and deny ourselves for the good of those whom we love. Love is sacrifice, love is self-giving, and love puts the beloved first.

If we want to sustain the feeling of love for our spouses, we must "fan the flames" with sacrificial acts of kindness, patience, and respect. And very often, these come more easily when we are understanding. Sometimes we place unfair expectations on our husbands. To begin with, we cannot expect our husbands to make us happy or fulfill us completely. Only God can do that. At times, we may have the tendency to expect our husbands to read our minds, and we sometimes become upset or irritated when they do not figure out what is bothering us. We need to communicate with charity, rather than leave our husbands mystified

---

4. Gerald Brenan, *St John of the Cross: His Life and Poetry*, (New York: Cambridge University Press, 1975), p. 74.

as to why we have suddenly grown cold on them. Praying
to our husband's guardian angels will also help us to communicate with kindness.

We need to understand that our husbands are wired
very differently than we are. God intended the differences
between a man and woman to be complementary, but
sometimes these differences can cause frictions. You may
be a very tidy person, but your husband may not notice
clutter. You may be a social butterfly, but your husband
may be more of a recluse. You may have a tendency to be
lenient with your children, but your husband may be quite
strict. Rather than expecting our husbands to conform
themselves to our ways of doing things and our ways of
thinking, we need to accept these differences and foster a
deep respect for them. Often, when these differences seem
like polar opposites, they can actually create a healthy bal-
ance for our children, but only if both spouses treat each
other with respect and understanding.

Let us ask the Holy Spirit to deepen the gift of understanding, which He bestowed upon us when we received
the sacrament of Confirmation. From understanding flows
patience, kindness, and respect. And these, in turn, enable
us to love our husbands actively and faithfully, strengthen-
ing the bonds of our marriage and family.

Patience with Ourselves

The wise and gentle St. Francis de Sales wrote:

> Know that the virtue of patience is that which secures
> us the greatest perfection; and if we must have patience
> with others, we must also have it with ourselves. Those

who aspire to the pure love of God have more need of patience with themselves than with others.[5]

Having patience with ourselves requires humility and trust because it means we have to understand our own limitations and imperfections and place them in the hands of God. Unless we are humbly patient with ourselves, we are likely to be exacting, demanding, and insensitive toward others. Even more, we will exhaust and stress ourselves in our futile attempt to be the inflated version of the person our pride makes us think we must be.

One day I saw a sign that made me laugh. The sign bore the bright red and yellow Superman logo, and it read:

Super Mom

Super Wife

Super Woman

Super Tired.

So many of us mothers place the burden of unrealistic expectations on ourselves. I think this is partly because we long for our children to have the very best we can give them. We worry about their education. We want to give them the best possible start in life, and we can wear ourselves out trying to do so. I also think we tend to place unrealistic expectations on ourselves because of the modern notion that the liberated woman can "do it all" and "have it all."

Indeed, mothers of today play many roles: teacher, cook, housekeeper, driver, household accountant, laundry lady,

---

5. St. Francis de Sales, *The Consoling Thoughts of St. Francis de Sales*, gathered from his writing and arranged in order by the Rev. Pere Huguet, translated from the Seventh French Edition, (Dublin: M.H. Gill & Son 1877), p. 126.

nurse, volunteer, and of course, there is the energy-zapping job of being a baby incubator if you are pregnant, and the part-time or full-time jobs that many mothers work at in or outside of the home. With so much work to do, there is certainly a lot of pressure to be Super Woman. And yet, when we try to be Super Woman, we often end up burnt out, weary, moody, and discouraged.

Again, the solution is only to be found in prayer. We need to pray to God for faith in his providence and his plan for each of our children and for our families. We need to trust that we don't need to work ourselves to utter exhaustion in order for his holy will to be done in our children's lives. And we need to pray for the wisdom to know which activities are God's will and which activities are burdens we place on ourselves due to materialism, pride, or fear. We can only know this through prayer. Without prayer, we navigate through all our decision-making spiritually blindfolded. Without prayer, we flub our way through each day, lacking wisdom and guidance from the Holy Spirit. Through prayer, God gives us light, clarity, purpose, and direction. With his insights, we can know his will and find peace in doing it because doing his will is all that really matters.

Blessed Luigi Orione enjoins us to keep our hearts fixed on prayer:

> Without Prayer nothing good is done. God's works are done with our hands joined, and on our knees. Even when we run, we must remain spiritually kneeling before Him.[6]

---

6. Terry R. Lynch, *Prayer: Teach Us to Pray*, (CreateSpace Independent Publishing Platform, 2013), p. 48.

Likewise, St. Charles Borromeo maintains:

> We must meditate before, during and after everything
> we do. The prophet says: "I will pray, and then I will
> understand." This is the way we can easily overcome
> the countless difficulties we have to face day after day,
> which, after all, are part of our work: in meditation we
> find the strength to bring Christ to birth in ourselves
> and in other men.[7]

If we are to have realistic expectations of ourselves, we also need to understand our personal limitations. When a toddler is unusually cranky, we often say, "He needs a nap." or "He must be really hungry." Well, it so happens that the same is true for most adults! Some people become very cantankerous when their stomachs are rumbling. Others, like myself, find it extremely difficult to be cheerful and patient when they are very tired. Out of charity for others, we should try to avoid reaching the point of hunger or fatigue such that we become irritable and unpleasant. One year, my sister decided to give up her daily coffee for Lent. After a few days, the headaches caused by caffeine withdrawal were so painful and she was so miserable that her six-year-old son suggested she give up wine instead. "My giving up coffee turned out to be a sacrifice for everyone," she said. So drink the coffee, eat the snack, take that nap. Know your limitations, and for the sake of charity, do what it takes to be kind and patient with your family.

As for our personal defects and weaknesses, we need to be humbly aware of them but never become complacent

---

7. Excerpt from a sermon by Saint Charles Borromeo: *Acta Ecclesiae Mediolanensis*, (Mediolani 1599), 1177–1178. Catholic Church, *The Liturgy of the Hours According to the Roman Rite*, 1975, v. 4, Nov. 4, "The Office of Readings," p.1545.

or discouraged by them. Complacency is the work of the devil, who wants us to give up striving for virtue and holiness. "So you're moody. That's just the way you are. Your kids and husband will just have to put up with you." Discouragement is what the devil uses to trick us into believing that we are not cut out for the work God has given us. "What makes you think that you will be able to continue homeschooling? You're so impatient! You're always losing your temper with your kids. You'll ruin them for life. You may as well give up."

Instead of giving into complacency or discouragement, we need to work on overcoming our faults with patience and perseverance, trusting that God will work through our imperfections. A friend of mine told me that her constant prayer is "Lord, make my children saints in spite of my shortcomings. Dear God, make up for all that I am lacking." Our humble awareness of our faults should impel us to cast ourselves onto God's mercy. Then, with St. Paul, we can joyfully and confidently say:

> But he said to me, "My grace is sufficient for you, for my power is made perfect in weakness." I will all the more gladly boast of my weaknesses, that the power of Christ may rest upon me. For the sake of Christ then, I am content with weaknesses, insults, hardships, persecutions, and calamities; for when I am weak, then I am strong.[8]

And with St. Thérèse, proclaim: "Oh! How happy I am to see myself imperfect and be in need of God's mercy!"[9]

---

8. 2 Cor 12:9–10.

9. St. Thérèse of Lisieux, *Story of a Soul*, third edition translated from the original manuscripts by John Clarke, O.C.D. (Washington D.C.: ICS Publications, 1996), p. 267.

The Patience of God

Finally, when we feel impatient with our children, we'll do well to remember the infinite patience of God. We can see God's marvelous and loving patience through salvation history. He waited seventy-five generations after the fall of Adam for his Son to come down to earth and offer himself up in atonement for our sins. During this time, God lovingly and patiently prepared the Israelites for the coming of the Messiah. As much as his Chosen People grieved him with their infidelity and ingratitude, our Lord never gave up on them. He never lost patience with them.

Our loving Father extends this same patience to us on a personal level. Mercifully in the sacrament of confession, he forgives us our sins, no matter how often we repeat them, as long as our contrition is sincere. So when our children test our patience and we want to roll our eyes and say, "When will you *ever* learn to brush your teeth without being told?" or "When will you kids *finally* stop bickering?," let's pause and remember how patient is our Lord with our own imperfections and our own slow progress in overcoming them. Praying for wisdom and understanding, we will strive to imitate our Lord in his patience, mercy, and love.

7.

A Heart Pierced with Sorrow

> Let us bind ourselves tightly to the Sorrowful Heart of
> our Heavenly Mother and reflect on its boundless grief
> and how precious is our soul.
>
> — St. Padre Pio[1]

" If only I had a heart like the Blessed Mother's," I used
to tell myself. "I would be a much better mother and
wife." *Mary, make my heart like yours!* Kind, gentle, pure,
patient, loving, serene . . . this is Mary's heart, adorned
with all the fruits of the Spirit. How wonderful it would
be to have a heart like Mary's! She is the perfect model
for all mothers, and we should try to imitate her in all her
virtues. But above all, we should try to imitate her in her
deep love for God and in her loving and prayerful acceptance of the sufferings and sorrows that she had to endure.

Sometimes we can look at Mary and think that she had
it easy and that maybe she can't really relate to us. After
all, conceived without sin, she was perfectly good without effort. She had all the virtues in perfection. She never
had to struggle to control her temper or bite her tongue to

---

1. "Counsels and Exhortations By Saint Padre Pio," *http://solinger.com/saint
padrepio/counsels-by-padre-pio.pdf*.

keep back unkind words. She was married to St. Joseph, the most saintly husband who ever lived. They probably never fought. And her son never had a meltdown, never disobeyed her, never said a disrespectful word, always cleaned up his room, and was the brightest child in his class. No wonder Mary was always so serene! *Blessed art thou among women!*

And yet, the three brief passages in the Bible that speak of Mary's heart describe it as only two things: pierced with sorrow and contemplative. We first read about Mary's heart at the end of the Nativity story.

> When the angels went away from them into heaven, the shepherds said to one another, "Let us go over to Bethlehem and see this thing that has happened, which the Lord has made known to us." And they went with haste, and found Mary and Joseph, and the babe lying in a manger. And when they saw it they made known the saying which had been told them concerning this child; and all who heard it wondered at what the shepherds told them. But Mary kept all these things, pondering them in her heart."[2]

When Mary and Joseph brought the infant Jesus to be presented in the Temple, an upright and devout man named Simeon prophesied to Mary: "*A sword will pierce through your own soul.*"[3] Years later, when Jesus was twelve, he went with his parents on a pilgrimage back to the Temple in Jerusalem. On their way home, Mary and Joseph realized that he was not with their caravan. For

---

2. Lk 2:15–20.
3. Lk 2:35.

three days, they searched Jerusalem and finally found him in the temple among the teachers.

> And when they saw him they were astonished; and his mother said to him, "Son, why have you treated us so? Behold, your father and I have been, looking for you anxiously." And he said to them, "How is it that you sought me? Did you not know that I must be in my Father's house?" And they did not understand the saying which he spoke to them.
>
> And he went down with them and came to Nazareth, and was obedient to them; and his mother kept all these things in her heart.[4]

Simeon's prophecy comes true. As we read and meditate on the life of Christ, we see that more than anything, Mary's heart is a heart of sorrow and of prayer.

Mary's heart was pierced not only once, but according to tradition, seven times. In the Bible, the number seven represents completion or perfection, and indeed, the sufferings of Mary encompass the most poignant sorrows a mother could ever endure. The seven sorrows of Mary are as follows:

1. The Prophecy of Simeon (Luke 2:34–35)
2. The Flight into Egypt (Matthew 2:13–15)
3. The Loss of the Child Jesus in the Temple (Luke 2:41–51)
4. The Meeting of Jesus and Mary on the Way of the Cross (Luke 2:25–35;)
5. The Crucifixion (Luke 23:27–31)

---

4. Lk 2:48–51.

6. The Taking Down of the Body of Jesus from the Cross (John 19:38–40)

7. The Burial of Jesus (Mark 15:46–47)

The Presentation of Jesus in the Temple is one of the Joyful Mysteries of the Rosary, yet it quickly becomes a moment of sorrow when Simeon makes his prophesy.

> Behold, this child is set for the fall and rising of many in Israel, and for a sign that is spoken against (and a sword will pierce through your own soul also), that thoughts out of many hearts may be revealed. (Luke 2:34–35)

Knowledge of certain future suffering is a sorrow that our Blessed Mother understands deeply. It is the suffering of a mother who finds out her child has a serious medical condition. It is the anxiety of a wife who learns that her husband is about to lose his job. Our Blessed Mother had perfect trust in God, but that did not spare her from the very human conditions of worry and anxiety.

Contemplating The Flight into Egypt, one can easily imagine the fear that clutched Mary's heart as the Holy family fled from the murderous hands of Herod into a foreign land of strange tongues and false gods. In this, the Blessed Mother experienced the pitiful plight of the refugee. She knows the homesickness of the poor and lonely immigrant. She understands the agony of a mother who fears for the life of her baby, born or unborn.

Perhaps one of the most dreadful experiences a parent can have is for his or her child to go missing. Imagine the alarm and the increasing desperation with which Joseph and Mary ran through the streets of Jerusalem, crying out Jesus' name. Remembering that they had fled to Egypt when Jesus was a baby, perhaps Joseph and Mary wondered if Jesus had been kidnapped or had fallen into the hands of evildoers. Perhaps they felt remorse for not keeping a closer eye on Jesus, even if he was, at twelve years old, very responsible and mature. And so Mary knows the terror of losing a child. Having a teenage or adult child who is spiritually lost and who has strayed from the Church is a source of great consternation and sorrow for parents who value their faith. We can always turn to Mary for her powerful intercession on behalf of children who are lost souls, living lives of immorality and self-destructive behavior. Surely, she will draw forth God's mercy and the grace of conversion if we persist in our prayers with faith and trust.

One of the hardest things about having children who persist in leading immoral lives is that we see them suffer and, aside from praying, there is very little we can do to help. How heartbreaking it is to watch your child struggle and not be able to do anything about it! Imagine Mary's sorrow, then, as she sees her beloved son, scourged and bleeding profusely, struggling to drag the heavy cross while soldiers beat him with whips. If only she could gather him in her arms, wipe away the blood, and hold him in a loving embrace, whispering sweet words, as she had done when he'd been a child! But now, all she can do is gaze upon him with the most profound compassion and love, uniting her sorrow to his. When we feel utterly helpless in the face of our children's sufferings, Mary knows and understands. She is ready to hold us in her arms and console us, if only we let her.

Mary watched her beloved son, bruised, bloody, and battered, drag the cross up to Calvary. And then, as if that wasn't enough, Mary saw the soldiers strip Christ of all his garments and nail him to the cross. The pounding of the hammer on the nails that pierced Jesus' sacred hands pounded painfully on her heart. She could never forget the sound of metal on metal, nor the look of her shaking, writhing son as he endured, for love of us, wave upon wave of excruciating pain. After Christ died, "one of the soldiers pierced his side with a spear, and at once there came out blood and water."[5] Although our Lord did not feel the pain of that wound, surely Mary felt searing pain in her heart. Standing at the foot of the cross during those final agonizing hours, Mary must have been far, far beyond her threshold for pain and suffering. Were it not for the grace of God, she would have died from grief because her suffering, intensified by perfect love, was more than any human could bear.

There will be times when we, too, will be taken beyond our threshold of suffering. There will be times when we will have to endure what we thought was unimaginable, impossible, and unbearable. When it seems that we must die from grief, Mary is with us, obtaining from God the grace to continue on.

Right before he died, our Lord cried out, "My God, my God, why hast thou forsaken me?"[6] United with her son in his sufferings and Passion, did Our Lady feel forsaken too? At least once before in her life, she had not understood God's plan. When the child Jesus had told Mary and Joseph in the temple, "Did you not know I must be in my Father's house?" she had not understood what he

---

5. Jn 19:34.
6. Mt 27:46.

meant. Perhaps there were other times, too, when God's plan seemed incomprehensible, as when Joseph could not find a decent place for Mary to give birth, or when they had to flee to Egypt. When Mary cradled her dead son in her arms, did she feel, once again, that God's plan was an utter mystery? Holding the lifeless and precious body of her adorable son, did Mary relive those moments when she and Joseph had not been able to make sense of the events in Jesus' life that seemed so incongruous to the One who was to be the Messiah?

In his beautiful Pietà, the famous marble statue of Mary holding the dead body of her crucified son, Michelangelo gives Mary a beautiful expression of perfect serenity. Despite the intensity of her grief, she submits her will to the will of God with complete and perfect trust. Often, in our own sorrows, we rant and rave because we do not understand how God could allow such terrible suffering. We need to learn from Mary that peace does not come from understanding God's will. Rather, peace comes from accepting and embracing God's will, which is always loving, always merciful, and always pointing to our salvation.

Alone. After the soldiers rolled the stone over Jesus' grave, Mary must have felt incredibly alone. A widow and now a mother whose only son was a condemned criminal, Mary would be a social outcast, scorned and rejected by neighbors and perhaps even relatives. But she would feel alone, especially because her beloved Son, the light of her eyes and the joy of her heart, lay buried in the tomb. John will take her into his home and care for her as if she is his own mother, and the other apostles and holy women will treat her with great affection and reverence. For this she will feel grateful and will bring down a thousand graces upon them. But even this most loving care is nothing compared to a glance, a smile, a cherished word from her beloved son. Her heart is like an empty tomb, wherein lies only utter loneliness. You mothers and fathers, who know the unspeakable anguish of burying a child or a spouse, seek solace in the heart of Mary. Let her weep with you, and you weep with her. And in her pierced and loving heart, you will find peace and consolation and the strength of hope in life beyond death.

These are the sorrows of Mary, God's favored one. Foreknowledge of certain suffering, having to flee from a murderous ruler and live in a foreign land, feeling anxiety and fear for her lost child, enduring social condemnation and humiliation, having to stand by and watch the brutal death of her son, experiencing the loneliness and grief of a widow burying her only child. Sorrow upon sorrow pierced her immaculate heart, and yet she remained faithful in her love for God, constantly united to him in prayer. Mary, the model of all Christian mothers, understands deeply our own sufferings. We will know peace as we seek her intercession for the grace to emulate her in all her virtues, especially that of being faithful in suffering. For then we will have a heart like hers.

8.

Faithfulness and Joy
in Suffering

"The violence of the blows that had struck my father
had opened up immense spiritual depths in him; his
grief found its outlet in prayer. The mere fact of seeing
him on his knees in prayer had a decisive influence on
my early years."

— St. John Paul II[1]

One of the most important lessons we can teach our children is how to endure suffering with faith, hope, and love, because suffering is an inevitable part of life. At some point in their lives, our children will have to endure great suffering. What a grace it is to know how to cope with suffering without losing one's faith, and better yet, to be able to embrace suffering as spiritual treasure. But we can only teach them this through our own heroic example of faith and even joy in the face of tribulations and sorrow.

Meditating on the seven sorrows of our Blessed Mother is a beautiful source of spiritual strength because it teaches

---

1. Renzo Allegri, *John Paul II: A Life of Grace*, (Cincinnati: St. Anthony Messenger Press, 2005), p. 39.

us how to endure and embrace even the most grievous sufferings. Mary, like her son Jesus, never committed a sin in
her life. Her heart was immaculate and full of complete
and perfect goodness. Why, then, did she suffer so much?
It was not through any fault of her own but in order to be
united to the sufferings of her son—and thus pay the price
for our sins. Christ, through his Passion and death on the
cross, redeemed us from our sins. Mary, in uniting her sufferings to the sufferings of Christ on the cross, became our
co-redemptrix.

Like Mary, we can unite our sufferings to the sufferings of Christ. Suffering, when it is lovingly united to the
cross of Christ, is never senseless or pointless. Rather, our
crosses become spiritual jewels with which we can make
reparation for our sins and ransom the souls of those
whom we love. Said Blessed Anthony Chevrier, "You teach
souls by word. You save them by suffering."[2]

Christ himself spoke of this to St. Faustina: "You will
save more souls through prayer and suffering than will a
missionary through his teaching and sermons alone."[3]

And St. Teresa of Calcutta, whose ministry revolved
around the suffering, noted:

> Suffering is a sign—a sign that we have come so close
> to Jesus on the cross that he can kiss us, show us that
> he is in love with us by giving us an opportunity to
> share in his Passion. Suffering is not a punishment,
> nor a fruit of sin; it is a gift of God. He allows us to

2. http://www.catholictradition.org/Passion/passion13.htm.

3. Christopher Osita Ezeh, *Holy Eucharist: The Beauty of Catholicism and the Glory and Essence of the Catholic Priesthood; The Scandal of its Abuses*, (Blooming-ton, Ind.: Author House, 2014), p. 158.

share in his suffering and to make up for the sins of the world.[4]

Fatigue, aches and pains, allergies, stress at home or work, financial worries, grief and sorrow—when we offer these up to our Lord as a sacrifice of love, our sufferings take on redemptive value. Knowing that we can use our sufferings to win souls for heaven, we can more easily embrace our crosses with love and joy. Our sufferings, instead of making us resentful, angry, and bitter, can teach us to be patient, compassionate, humble, and grateful. "If we only knew the precious treasure hidden in infirmities," wrote St. Vincent de Paul. "we would receive them with the same joy with which we receive the greatest benefits. And we would bear them without ever complaining or showing signs of weariness."[5]

We parents often think nothing of the sacrifices we make for our children in order for them to have a comfortable home, to receive a solid education, or to enjoy small pleasures. We work long hours to put food on the table and stay up all night to care for a sick child. And we usually think very little of it, even though the sacrifice is great. Why? Because we love. Love transforms a sacrifice so that it is no longer a sacrifice, but a joyful means to a desirable end. Love is the honey in a bitter drink, bringing sweetness to sacrifice. The more we love our children, the more we are willing to suffer for them. And the more we suffer for our children, the more we grow in love for them.

---

4. Mother Teresa, *Where There is Love, There is God: Her Path to Closer Union with God and Greater Love for Others*, (Crown Publishing Group, 2010), p. 335.

5. *The Liguorian*, Vol. 43, (Redemptorists, 1955), p. 697.

The same is true in our relationship with Christ. The more we love our Lord, the more we are willing to suffer for him. The more we suffer for his sake, the more we grow in love for him. And so, our Lord allows us to suffer to make reparation for our sins, to redeem the souls of others, and so that we might grow in love.

"Suffering is a great grace; through suffering the soul becomes like the Saviour; in suffering love becomes crystallized; the greater the suffering, the purer the love."

—St. Faustina[6]

When Jesus suffered and died on the cross, He not only redeemed us, He also showed us the way to love: "Greater love has no man than this, that a man lay down his life for his friends."[7]

St. Gemma Galgani learned this from our Lord himself:

One evening when I was at prayer he came to bring peace to my soul. I felt myself entirely recollected and I found myself for a second time before Jesus Crucified. He said to me: "Look daughter, and learn how to love," and He showed me His five open wounds. "Do you see this cross, these thorns, these nails, these bruises, these tears, these wounds, this blood? They are all works of love; of infinite love. Do you see how much I have loved you? Do you really want to love Me? Then first learn to suffer. It is by suffering that one learns to love."[8]

---

6. St. Maria Faustina Kowalska, *Diary of Saint Maria Faustina Kowalska*, (Stockbridge: Marian Press, 2005), p. 39, no. 57.

7. Jn 15:13.

8. St. Gemma Galgani, *The Autobiography of St. Gemma Galgani*, (London: Catholic Way Publishing, 1st Edition), p. 44.

This is one reason why the saints prized suffering so highly.

"Thank the good God for having visited you through suffering; if we knew the value of suffering, we would ask for it."

—St. Andre[9]

"Suffering is a great favor."

—St. Teresa of Avila[10]

Because suffering, when united to Christ's cross, causes us to grow in love, it is also a sign of God's favor and closeness.

"We always find that those who walked closest to Christ Our Lord were those who had to bear the greatest trials."

—St. Teresa of Avila[11]

"[We] consider tribulation as a gracious gift of God, a gift that he specially gave his special friends."

—St. Thomas More[12]

"When we are in tribulation, it is necessary to be more happy and more joyful, because one is nearer to God."

—St. Clare of Assisi[13]

9. Ronda Chervin, *Quotable Saints*, (CMJ Publishers, 2003), p. 33.

10. St. Teresa of Avila, *The Collected Letters of St. Teresa of Avila: 1578–1582* (Washington, DC: ICS Publications, 2001), p. 334.

11. St. Teresa of Avila, *Interior Castle* (Mineola, N.Y.: Dover, 2012), p. 163.

12. St. Thomas More, *Dialogue of Comfort Against Tribulation: with Modifications to Obsolete Language*, ed. Monica Stevens, (The Floating Press, 2013), p. 84.

13. Ronda Chervin, *Quotable Saints*, (Oaklawn, Ill.: CMJ Marian, 1992), p. 174.

"If God causes you to suffer much, it is a sign that He has great designs for you, and that He certainly intends to make you a saint."

—St. Ignatius of Loyola[14]

We see the truth of this in our Blessed Mother, who was closer to Christ than any human being, and yet whose profound suffering, except for the sufferings of her son, remain unparalleled. Mary is the most blessed among women and the most highly favored among women because of her capacity to love, and, therefore, her capacity to suffer for love.

Sometimes our Lord pierces our hearts with sorrows so severe that we are left reeling in pain and aghast that God could allow such things to happen. The death of a child or spouse, terminal illness, a chronic and debilitating disease that knows no cure, infertility, the breakup of a marriage, extreme poverty, or a child who is addicted to drugs or alcohol and seems bent on going down the road to destruction. These tremendously heavy crosses often threaten to crush our faith in God's goodness or power. As we move through the various stages of grief, we may wonder: *How can God possibly be good or loving? How can he allow this? Is he really all-powerful? Is he really in control? Why my family? And why doesn't God answer my prayers?*

Understanding the reasons for our suffering may come in time, or it may not. Often, like a newborn who screams in pain when a doctor pricks his heel and squeezes out the blood, drop by painful drop, to test for jaundice, we

14. Benedict J. Groeschel and John Bishop, *There are No Accidents: In All Things Trust in God*, (Huntington, Ind.: Our Sunday Visitor Publishing, 2004), p. 85.

are incapable of understanding the reasons for our suffering. For our understanding is nothing compared to the infinite wisdom of God the Creator, who sees all time, knows all things, and understands how every event in our lives affects our futures, the lives of others, and all of humanity.

And so we need to trust. We need to trust that our suffering is part of God's loving plan. We need to trust that God is in control, that he knows what he is doing, and that this suffering is ultimately an act of mercy and love which will draw us closer to him.

"For as the heavens are higher than the earth, so are my ways higher than your ways and my thoughts higher than your thoughts."[15]

Yet trusting God in the face of extreme suffering is incredibly, vastly, tremendously difficult. *How is this suffering supposed to bring me closer to God? It's not! It's creating a rift between God and me. I can't believe that God is good or loving. My faith, if I had any, is smashed to smithereens. I'm so angry at God that I can't pray. I don't even want to pray! He hasn't answered my prayers, anyway.*

How well Job knew these feelings, as in the Book of Job, he laments:

[K]now then that God has put me in the wrong,
and closed his net around me.

Behold, I cry out, "Violence!" But I am not answered;
I call aloud, but there is no justice.[16]

---

15. Is 55:9.
16. Jb 19:6–7.

> God has cast me into the mire,
> and I have become like dust and ashes.
> I cry to thee and thou dost not answer me;
> I stand, and thou does not heed me."[17]

This is the anguished cry of Job, who, after his wealth and health had been taken away and his family had been killed, was told by his friends that he must have sinned grievously for God to have afflicted him so greatly. And yet Job was righteous, and God knew it.

God had given Job a test of faith. "Curse God, and die,"[18] Job's wife told him. But Job did not. Instead, he clung to God. Job was angry. Job did not understand God's purpose. But Job did not give up on God.

> Behold, he will slay me; I have no hope;
> yet I will defend my ways to his face.[19]

> For I know that my Redeemer lives,
> and at last he will stand upon the earth;
> and after my skin has been thus destroyed,
> then from my flesh I shall see God.[20]

Job had given up on all hopes of earthly happiness and had set his sights on heaven. But the Lord rewarded Job for his faithfulness, even on earth:

> And the Lord blessed the latter days of Job more than
> his beginning; and he had fourteen thousand sheep, six

---

17. Jb 30:19–20.
18. Jb 2:9.
19. Jb 13:15.
20. Jb 19:25–26.

thousand camels, a thousand yoke of oxen, and a thousand she-asses. He had also seven sons and three daughters. And he called the name of the first Jemi'mah; and the name of the second Kezi'ah; and the name of the third Ker'en-hap'puch. And in all the land there were no women so fair as Job's daughters; and their father gave them inheritance among their brothers. And after this Job lived a hundred and forty years, and saw his sons, and his sons' sons, four generations. And Job died, an old man, and full of days.[21]

When suffering causes you to undergo a trial of faith, and you feel as if you cannot pray, cannot trust, cannot endure any more, know for certain that you are not alone. You may feel as if there is a chasm between God and you, but he is closer to you than ever, for "The Lord is near to the broken-hearted, and saves the crushed in spirit."[22]

When you pass through the waters, I will be with you; and through the rivers, they shall not overwhelm you, when you walk through fire, you shall not be burned, and the flame shall not consume you.[23]

Do you remember the story of Jesus walking on the water?

And in the fourth watch of the night he came to them, walking on the sea. But when the disciples saw him walking on the sea, they were terrified, saying, "It is a ghost!" And they cried out for fear. But immediately he spoke to them, saying, "Take heart, it is I; have no fear."

---

21. Jb 42:12–17.
22. Ps 34:18.
23. Is 43:2.

And Peter answered him, "Lord, if it is you, bid me come to you on the water." He said, "Come." So Peter got out of the boat and walked on the water and came to Jesus; but when he saw the wind, he was afraid, and beginning to sink he cried out, "Lord, save me." Jesus immediately reached out his hand and caught him, saying to him, "O you of little faith, why did you doubt?" And when they got into the boat, the wind ceased. And those in the boat worshiped him, saying, "Truly you are the Son of God."[24]

Our tribulations are like the stormy winds. Trusting in God is like walking on water. Trusting in God when our lives are in turmoil can seem as impossible as walking on water. We can only do it with God's grace. Like Peter, we need to cry out to him for help. *Jesus put out his hand at once and held him.* Jesus held Peter, but Peter must have clung to Jesus, clutching onto him for dear life. When our faith is shaky, whenever we feel that we cannot trust, like Peter, we need to cling to Jesus and let Jesus hold us. Jesus will bring us to safety. He will calm the storm. And when the trial has passed, however long it may be, we will have a stronger faith than ever, just like the apostles, who after the winds had stopped, bowed down before him and said, "Truly, you are the Son of God."[25]

Not long after, in Capernaum, Jesus preached his Bread of Life discourse in which he told the Jews that he was the Bread of Life.

---

24. Mt 14:25–33.
25. Mt 14:33.

"I am the living bread which came down from heaven; if any one eats of this bread, he will live for ever; and the bread which I shall give for the life of the world is my flesh."[26]

When the Jews started arguing among themselves because they could not comprehend his words, Jesus affirmed his teaching:

"Truly, truly, I say to you, unless you eat the flesh of the Son of man and drink his blood, you have no life in you; he who eats my flesh and drinks my blood has eternal life, and I will raise him up at the last day. For my flesh is food indeed, and my blood is drink indeed. He who eats my flesh and drinks my blood abides in me, and I in him."[27]

It is easy to understand how the Jews felt: confounded, perplexed, even disgusted. After all, eating the flesh of another person is beyond barbaric; it is savage and beastly. No wonder many recoiled at this teaching, as evidenced by the following:

Many of his disciples, when they heard it, said, "This is a hard saying; who can listen to it?"[28]

After this, many of his disciples drew back and no longer went about with him.[29]

---

26. Jn 6:51–54.
27. Jn 6:53–56.
28. Jn 6:60.
29. Jn 6:66.

When we suffer a trial of faith, we too may feel like giving up on God. We need to imitate Peter, who again clung to Christ.

> Jesus said to the Twelve, "Will you also go away?" Simon Peter answered him, "Lord, to whom shall we go? You have the words of eternal life; and we have believed, and have come to know, that you are the Holy One of God."[30]

Very often, Peter and the other apostles did not understand the teachings of our Lord. Sometimes they had to ask Jesus to explain a parable. Other times, Peter's impetuous remonstrances to Jesus' words earned him reproaches from our Lord. Even in this case, when Jesus asks the apostles if they, like the unbelieving disciples, want to go away, Peter does not claim to understand our Lord's teaching. He does not understand, and he will not fully understand until the Last Supper and perhaps even Pentecost. His faith is being tested, but he clings to the Lord, cleaves to his trust in Jesus, and makes one of the most beautiful professions of faith recorded in the Bible.

In times of sorrow and doubt, we need to cling to Jesus with the childlike tenacity and persistence of Peter. How do we do this? In his *Spiritual Exercises*, St. Ignatius wrote fourteen rules for the Spiritual life. The fifth rule teaches us how to cling to Christ:

> In time of desolation never make a change, but be firm and constant in the proposals and determination in which one was the day preceding such desolation, or

---

30. Jn 6:67–69.

in the determination in which one was in the preceding consolation. Because, as in consolation the good spirit guides and counsels us more, so in desolation the bad spirit, with whose counsels we cannot find the way to a right decision.[31]

We cling to Jesus by being faithful to our spiritual practices. In times of great suffering, doubts will overwhelm and temptations will assault us. Seeing our weakened faith, the devil will launch attack after attack, inciting us to give up on our faith. This is why we must never make a change to our spiritual plan of life in a time of desolation. Rather, we must be steadfast and stalwart, in spite of how we feel.

Blessed is the man who endures trial, for when he has stood the test he will receive the crown of life which God has promised to those who love him.[32]

No matter how angry you are, keep on going to Mass, even if all you do is sit in the pew in stony silence. Persevere in your prayers, even if you feel you can't pray, or feel that your prayers are futile. You may think that your prayers are a waste of time because you feel that God doesn't listen to them. It only seems that way. God does listen, but he has better plans for you.

As parents, we know there are certain things we would never give to our children no matter how much they begged, pleaded, nagged, and cried for them. Do our children cut themselves off from us? They may stomp off to their rooms and sulk for a while, but they know how much

---

31. Fr. Timothy Gallagher, Spiritual Consolation: *An Ignatian Guide for the Greater Discernment Of Spirits*, (New York: Crossroad Publishing Co., 2005), p.131.

32. Jas 1:12.

they need us. Eventually, they come back, seeking our loving embrace. And we, sorry for their disappointment, find ways to console them.

God, our loving Father, always hears our prayers. He hears us when we storm heaven with prayers. He hears all the novenas we make, the Masses we offer up, the rosaries we recite. He sees the sacrifices we make for this intention or that. And he wants us to be happy. He desires our happiness more than we desire it ourselves. But sometimes what we beg, bargain, and plead for is really not what is best for our souls, or for the souls of those for whom we are praying. Why God allows a young mother to die of cancer, or a baby to be born with a fatal genetic disorder, is a mystery we will never be able to fathom during our lives on earth. Shaken as our faith is, we need to repeat those words of Peter, "Lord, to whom shall we go? You have the words of eternal life."[33]

In our suffering, we need God more than ever. And if we cling to him, he will console us and restore our faith, making it stronger than it ever was before.

So I urge you to persevere in your prayers. Remember that Mary's heart was sorrowful and prayerful. "His mother kept all these things in her heart"[34] Life is bound to give us sorrows, but it is our choice whether or not we pray through our sufferings.

Perhaps pain has numbed your mind and you cannot think, much less pray. Then set your eyes on a crucifix and simply gaze upon our Lord hanging in agony, as Mary did at the foot of the cross. Offer your sufferings to him and

---

33. Jn 6:67.
34. Lk 2:51.

let him behold your cross. Then words are not needed. In the words of St. Teresa of Avila:

> One must not think that a person who is suffering is not praying. He is offering up his sufferings to God, and many a time he is praying much more truly than one who goes away by himself, and meditates his head off, and if he has squeezed out a few tears, thinks that it is prayer.[35]

Similarly, St. Francis de Sales noted that, "One act performed in dryness of spirit is worth more than several done in great sensible fervor."[36] If you place yourself in the Presence of God and remain faithful to your prayers, even if you don't feel like it, even if you are angry or doubtful, God will give you consolation, hope, and yes, even joy.

One great source of consolation and strength is the prayers of friends and family. Especially during those times when you are strongly tempted to abandon your prayers, ask as many people as you can to pray for you. E-mail or text them if you can't bear to talk about it, but allow the prayers of others to sustain you. We were never meant to suffer alone, even if loneliness is part of our suffering. During his agony in the garden, Jesus repeatedly asked his apostles to stay awake and pray. Sadly, his apostles fell asleep, leaving him to feel more alone than ever, until an angel came to console Him. Jesus sets for us an example to ask for the prayers of others. If we do, in our hours of agony, God will send angels to console and sustain us.

---

35. *The Letters of Saint Teresa of Jesus*, Volume 1, ed. Edgar Allison Peers, (United Kingdom: Burns, Oates & Washbourne, 1966) p. 64.

36. Jean-Pierre Camus, Saint Francis de Sales, *The Spirit of S. Francis de Sales*, (Longmans, 1887), p. 65.

These angels may be friends or family members or sometimes unexpected people whom we "happen" to meet and who understand our sorrows deeply. They will pray for us and offer sacrifices for us, often more than we know. They can be a guiding light through the dark valley, offering hope and encouragement.

Even as he carried the cross to Calvary, Jesus met people along the way who offered him sympathy and love and who were sources of consolation: His Blessed Mother, St. Veronica, and the weeping women. And when Christ was barely able to carry on, Simon, a complete stranger, helped him carry his cross. In his final hours, Christ's Blessed Mother, St. John, and a handful of faithful friends courageously remained at the foot of the Cross. Their very presence was a prayer and an offering of love. As we carry our crosses, God will send people to us to support and console us. In our anger, we may want to push them away. Rather, with humility, great humility, we must let them minister to us, and know that even from a distance, they are praying for us.

One of the best things you can do when suffering causes you to undergo a trial of faith is to go to confession. In this sacrament of mercy, our Lord cleanses our souls and heals the wounds of our aching hearts. The healing power of confession is truly extraordinary. Pour out your anger, your doubts, and your feelings of helplessness, loneliness, and fear. And beg forgiveness for the times you acted on your anger, gave into temptations, or used your sufferings as a reason to justify your sins. The fastest way to learn to trust and accept God's will, to regain your peace, and to strengthen your faith is to reconcile with God and to bathe your soul in his mercy.

In Christ's words, spoken to St. Faustina:

Daughter, when you go to confession, to this fountain of My mercy, the Blood and Water which came forth from My Heart always flows down upon your soul and ennobles it. Every time you go to confession, immerse yourself entirely in My mercy, with great trust, so that I may pour the bounty of My grace upon your soul. When you approach the confessional, know this, that I Myself am waiting there for you. I am only hidden by the priest, but I Myself act in your soul. Here the misery of the soul meets the God of mercy.[37]

One day, I was reading the Gospel story of the widow's mite.

He looked up and saw the rich putting their gifts into the treasury; and he saw a poor widow put in two copper coins. And he said, "Truly I tell you, this poor widow has put in more than all of them; for they all contributed out of their abundance, but she out of her poverty put in all the living that she had."[38]

Somehow this gospel passage resonated with me. In the days that followed, this story came to my mind again and again. I was pregnant at the time and was full of fear and misgivings about the health of the baby. I wondered why the story haunted me, but my thoughts were mainly consumed with imploring our Lord to spare the life of the baby.

And then one Saturday evening, I began to bleed. Not a lot, but enough for fear to grip my heart. Sunday passed

---

37. Kowalska, 1602.
38. Luke 21:1–4.

in agonizing prayer. On Monday morning, I called the doctor and then went to Mass. When the priest began to read the Gospel, I began to weep. For he was reading the story of the widow's mite. And in a flash, I understood. I knew I was going to undergo a period of suffering, a time of severe spiritual poverty when all I could offer God was emptiness and tears. Later that day, an ultrasound confirmed my fears. I had miscarried a baby for the fourth time in a row.

The previous three miscarriages had been painful enough. I had mourned and grieved each loss for months. But the fourth left me feeling so far away from God, so forsaken, angry, betrayed, and hopeless that I wanted to abandon my faith. I could not believe in God's goodness or love. I stopped going to weekday Mass. I stopped praying the Rosary. I stopped teaching my kids religion. And I had to bite my tongue to hold back the sarcastic, caustic comments that came to mind about prayer and faith so I wouldn't scandalize the children. Plunged into spiritual darkness, I would not pray, could not pray. I had nothing to say to God.

But he had something to say to me:

Give me your widow's mite. Give me your nothingness, your emptiness. Give me your abject spiritual poverty, your doubts, your darkness, your anger, your broken heart. Your sorrows are worth more to me than your prayers said during sweet consolation or heroic deeds performed in moments of great faith. Give me your empty, aching heart, so I can fill it with my love. I long to transform your suffering into spiritual treasure. Only give me your poor, wounded heart.

Our Lord longs to heal our broken hearts with his love. He wants to transform our crosses into spiritual treasure to redeem souls and to purify and perfect our love for him. He can turn our doubts into strong, confident faith, our desolation into consolation, our anger and bewilderment into peace, and our sufferings into joy. Like a mother who yearns to comfort her distraught child, he reaches out his hands to hold us. All we need to do is cling to him until the storm dies down.

When we suffer, we should always keep in mind these eloquent words of St. John Vianney:

> Whether we will or not, we must suffer. There are some who suffer like the good thief, and others like the bad thief. They both suffered equally. But one knew how to make his sufferings meritorious, he accepted them in the spirit of reparation, and turning towards Jesus crucified, he received from His mouth these beautiful words: "This day thou shalt be with Me in Paradise." The other, on the contrary, cried out, uttered imprecations and blasphemies, and expired in the most frightful despair.
>
> There are two ways of suffering—to suffer with love, and to suffer without love. The saints suffered everything with joy, patience, and perseverance, because they loved. As for us, we suffer with anger, vexation, and weariness, because we do not love. If we loved God, we should love crosses, we should wish for them, we should take pleasure in them . . . We should be happy to suffer for the love of Him who lovingly suffered for us. Of what do we complain? Alas! The poor infidels, who have not the happiness of knowing God and his

infinite loveliness, have the same crosses that we have; but they have not the same consolations. You say it is hard? No, it is easy, it is consoling, it is sweet; it is happiness. Only we must love while we suffer, and suffer while we love.[39]

Our faithfulness to God in times of great suffering is one of the most powerful witnesses we can give our children. The life of St. John Paul II gives evidence of this. When he was only eight years old, his mother passed away. St. John Paul recalled his father's reaction:

After my mother's death, his life became one of constant prayer. Sometimes I would wake up during the night and find my father on his knees, just as I would always see him kneeling in the parish church.[40]

It was from his father that St. John Paul II learned to pray and to find consolation in prayer. Three years later, his father's example would teach him yet another invaluable lesson. His beloved older brother Edmund contracted scarlet fever and died. Broken hearted, yet full of faith, his father stood by the coffin repeating the words, "Thy will be done! Thy will be done!" This image and these words were engraved on St. John Paul II's memory in a most profound way. Years later, he often old friends that they had made a deep impact on him.[41]

Like the father of St. John Paul II, we can teach our children to suffer with love. St. John Paul II accomplished

---

39. *http://acatholiclife.blogspot.com/2006/08/catechism-on-suffering-by-st-john.html*.

40. Jason Evert, *Saint John Paul the Great: His Five Loves*, (Totus Tuus Press, 2014). p. 4.

41. Evert, pp. 4, 5.

many wonders and captivated millions of people around the world. But he was never so magnificent as when, ill with Parkinson's disease and bent with age, he showed the world the beauty, value, and dignity of suffering. Thank God for the quiet, heroic witness of his afflicted father! When God blesses us with suffering, may we too be examples of faithfulness, trust, and love. May our tears, mingled with our prayers, teach our children life's hardest yet greatest lesson: *to love while we suffer, and suffer while we love*. Then they, in their turn, can be joyful witnesses of God's unconditional love and mercy to their children, their children's children, and the world around them.

9.

Portals of Mercy

Let our judgment of souls cease, for God's mercy upon them is extraordinary.

—St. Faustina[1]

Finally, I would like to address that suffering which is the heartache of many devout parents: the sorrow caused by wayward children who abandon the practice of their faith or fall into grave sin. While the sin itself is a great evil, the suffering of the parents can be a blessing in disguise. For it allows us to understand and share more deeply in Christ's sorrow for our sins. Have you dedicated your life to the education and religious upbringing of your children, sparing no sacrifice to give them the best you possibly can? What desolation if or when one's child turns away from the faith and falls prey to the worldly enticements of sensuality, materialism, or false idealism! And a very painful rift in your relationship with your child very often accompanies this. Imagine then, the sorrowful and bleeding heart of Christ on the cross, who gave his very life for each one of us. And yet many still reject him! Our children's rebelliousness, disrespect, or lack of gratitude can make us poignantly aware of how our own sins and spiritual tepidity

1. Kowalska, 1684.

grieve the heart of our Heavenly Father. Our children's lack of repentance can draw us to deeper repentance; their lack of love should ignite in us a more ardent love. In this way, the pain of being estranged from our children can unite us ever more closely to the wounded heart of Christ.

When our hearts ache for our wayward children, we should remember the redemptive value of suffering. We should unite our sadness, anxiety, anger, and grief to our Lord's passion and offer it all up in reparation for the sins of our children. The sorrow of feeling that we are no longer able to help them because they reject our help and advice is perhaps the greatest help we can give them when we offer it all to Christ for their sake. Thus the sufferings our children cause us can serve as a ransom for their conversion. Let us not forget the spiritual treasure hidden in this suffering!

When children abandon their faith, many parents suffer from intense remorse or guilt over past failures or weaknesses. *If only I had spent more quality time with my family. If only I hadn't spoiled him so much. If only I hadn't let her go out with that guy. If only. . . .* And yet, if we have truly done our best to teach our children the faith, this remorse, albeit humbling, is unnecessary.

> The faults of children are not always imputed to the parents, especially when they have instructed them and given good example. Our Lord, in His wondrous Providence, allows children to break the hearts of devout fathers and mothers. Thus the decisions your children have made don't make you a failure as a parent in God's eyes. You are entitled to feel sorrow, but not necessarily guilt.[2]

2. Vincent J. O'Malley, *Ordinary Suffering of Extraordinary Saints*, (Huntington, Ind.: Our Sunday Visitor Publishing, 1999), pp. 92–93.

St. Louise de Marillac wrote this from experience. Her only son, Michel Antoine, was a source of great consternation and misery. When he was twenty-six, pushed by his mother, he received minor orders, a status of clergy below the rank of deacon. Antoine never felt certain that he really had a vocation to the priesthood, however, and not long after, he left the seminary. He adopted a lifestyle which led him to become involved in "scandalous situations." Angry at St. Louise, he stopped practicing his faith. Antoine then eloped and married a woman from the province, leaving his distraught mother in the dark as to his whereabouts.[3]

We should never assume that if we do everything right, our children will walk the straight and narrow path. St. Louise de Marillac had done all she could to raise Michel in the faith. After St. Louise's husband died, St. Vincent de Paul had "played a very important role in Michel's education . . . and became a father figure for him."[4] Nonetheless, despite having both a saintly mother and a saintly father-figure, Michel went astray.

Even our Lord, who was perfectly loving, had the sorrow of seeing two of his beloved disciples sin against him: Peter denied knowing him, and Judas betrayed Him. Did Jesus make a mistake? Should he have spent more quality time with Judas, or been a better example for Peter? Of course not! So, if saints have children who make sinful decisions and if even our Lord had apostles who made sinful decisions, we should not dare to presume that our children will never fall into grave sin.

---

3. Sr. Maria Teresa Barbero Echavarria, DC, *Saint Louise de Marillac and Education*. *http://famvin.org/wiki/Saint_Louise_de_Marillac_and_Education*.

4. Echavarria.

This is a scary, heart-breaking thought, but also a liberating one. For, as long as we have been faithful to our responsibility in educating our children in the Faith, we do not have to beat ourselves up with guilt and remorse if they fall into sinful ways. Rather, with faith, hope, and trust, we should place our children into God's loving and merciful hands, as did St. Louise.

She never gave up praying for her son. Rather, she made a pilgrimage to Chatres where she placed Antoine's soul into the care of Our Blessed Mother. Still suffering from guilt and worry two years later, St. Louise made an act of renunciation, completely surrendering her son to God. It was a tremendous act of faith and trust. As a result, Our Lord gave her the grace of acceptance, and with it a serenity of heart and a greater freedom of spirit.[5]

Trusting in God's mercy when our children's souls are in peril is a tremendous act of faith. It is one of the hardest things a parent can be called to do, and yet it is precisely what Our Lord calls us to do in situations such as these. Like St. Louise, we need to surrender our control over the situation and entrust our children entirely into the hands of Our Lady and the mercy of God. And the extent to which we trust in God's mercy for our children is often the extent of our peace and serenity in these difficult circumstances.

Both Judas and Peter sinned grievously against Our Lord and both suffered bitter remorse for what they had done. The difference between them was that Peter trusted in the mercy of God whereas Judas despaired of it. Judas, who had heard the story of the Prodigal Son from Jesus' own lips, who was present when Jesus forgave the

---

5. Echavarria.

adulterous woman and saved her from stoning, who had seen him perform countless acts of love and mercy, refused to believe that Jesus would have mercy on him. The sin that ultimately destroyed Judas was not his betrayal of Jesus. It was his lack of trust in God's mercy.

No matter how heinous our children's sins are, we must never despair of God's mercy for our children. We must hold fast to the hope that God will answer our prayers for our children's repentance and conversion. We must remain firm in the conviction that God's plans for our children can still come to fruition and that he can use even their erroneous ways for their sanctification.

St. Louise's prayers were answered. After two years, Michel "recovered his sense"[6] and reconciled with his mother. He eventually married and had a daughter who became a great source of joy and comfort for St. Louise. Like St. Louise, we need to pray and wait. It may take years or decades. You may not live to see the conversion of your wayward child. Still, we must trust in the power of Our Lady's intercession and in God's mercy for us and for our children.

We would do well to take the advice of St. Louise:

> Do not cease praying for your children; God's grace can touch a hardened heart. Commend your children to the Immaculate Heart of Mary. When parents pray the Rosary, at the end of each decade they should hold the Rosary aloft and say to her, "With these beads bind my children to your Immaculate Heart." She will attend to their souls.[7]

---

6. Echavarria.

7. O'Malley, pp. 92–93.

While we pray, wait, and offer up our sufferings for our children, we must be portals of God's mercy. When they were young, our children's first experiences of God's love were through us. Now, we must let them experience God's mercy through us. However angry we may feel, we must never alienate our adult children by our own unwillingness to forgive. On the one hand, we should not water down the teachings of the Church in order to accommodate or justify their lifestyles. On the other hand, we must avoid harsh judgments and condemnations. At times we will be called to speak the truth in charity; at other times we will need to suffer in prayerful silence. At all times, we must make it clear to our children, more often by example than by word, that in confession God is ever ready to forgive the repentant sinner and that his mercy knows no bounds.

Messages from the saints teach us of Christ's immeasurable mercy. Said Christ to St. Faustina:

[Let] the greatest sinners place their trust in My mercy. They have the right before others to trust in the abyss of My mercy. My daughter, write about My mercy towards tormented souls. Souls that make an appeal to My mercy delight Me. To such souls I grant even more graces than they ask. I cannot punish even the greatest sinner if he makes an appeal to My compassion, but on the contrary, I justify him in My unfathomable and inscrutable mercy. Write: before I come as a just judge, I first open wide the door of My mercy. He who refuses to pass through the door of My mercy must pass through the door of My justice . . .[8]

8. Kowalska, 1146.

And St. Isidore of Seville assured us:

> Confession heals, confession justifies, confession grants pardon of sin. All hope consists in confession. In confession there is a chance for mercy. Believe it firmly. Do not doubt, do not hesitate, never despair of the mercy of God. Hope and have confidence in confession.[9]

Difficult as it may be, we must try to imitate our Lord in his unfathomable mercy. Like the father of the Prodigal Son, we must be ready to welcome our children back with outstretched arms. He will give us the grace and strength to be merciful towards our children if we ask for it.

As much as their sins grieve him, our Lord has a tender, longing love for those who have strayed from the faith. This is why, "where sin increased, grace abounded all the more."[10] Although we may not see it, and very often we don't, our Lord is working on the souls of our errant children, seeking them and calling to them. St. Augustine spoke to this when he wrote:

> You called me; you cried aloud to me; you broke my barrier of deafness. You shone upon me; your radiance enveloped me; you put my blindness to flight. You shed your fragrance about me; I drew breath and now I gasp for your sweet odour. I tasted you, and now I hunger and thirst for you. You touched me, and I am inflamed with love of your peace.[11]

---

9. Johnnette S. Benkovic, *Confession: The Sacrament of Mercy and Healing*, (Huntington, Ind.: Our Sunday Visitor, 2001) 119.

10. Rom 5:20.

11. St. Augustine of Hippo, *Confessions*, translated by R.S. Pine-Coffin, (London: Penguin Classics, 1961), p. 232.

Such conversions are not a thing of the past. I have a relative who recently went to confession for the first time in fifty years. For twenty-five of those years, his wife faithfully prayed for his return to the sacraments. Even more, God continues to pursue souls even until the moment of death. Here's an example: I have a friend who ministers to prisoners in his local jail. One of the men he counseled had a conversion while in jail and returned to the practice of his faith. When the inmate had served his time, he was released from jail and he began going to church. But it wasn't long before he fell into crime and found himself behind bars. Again my friend ministered to him. Eventually, the man was released. Shortly after, my friend was devastated to hear that he had been killed in a car accident. He worried about the state of the ex-prisoner's soul. A few days later, he went to church, still upset over the sudden death of a man who had been faltering in his faith. But there he learned something that filled him with joy and amazement. The ex-convict had been killed in a car accident after leaving the church. Just prior to that, however, he had yielded to the mercy of God, gone to confession, and received Holy Communion! See how lovingly relentless is the mercy of God!

Each soul, for whom Christ suffered and died on the cross, is infinitely precious to our Heavenly Father. And so our Lord never gives up trying to draw souls to his Sacred Heart. He never ceases to offer his graces. Even until death, he offers his grace, his love, his mercy and forgiveness. As our Lord never gives up, neither must we. So, *"Wait for the Lord; be strong and take heart and wait for the Lord."*[12]

12. Ps 27:14.

The history of the Church gives us many examples of
great sinners who turned their lives around after experiencing the life-changing love and mercy of God. We can
think of Mary Magdalen, the adulteress possessed by
seven demons. Her experience of Jesus' love and mercy
so changed her heart that she had the courage and love
to remain at the foot of the Cross, even though all the
apostles except St. John had fled. After the Resurrection,
it was she who was an apostle to the apostles, announcing
to them the news that Jesus had risen from the dead. And
then there was St. Paul, the vehement persecutor of Christians who approved of the stoning of St. Stephen. After his
conversion, he became a tireless missionary whose inspired
writings became a significant part of the New Testament.
Many of us are familiar with St. Augustine, the brilliant
but proud scholar who, to his mother's sorrow, rejected
the Christian faith and became a Manichaean pagan living
a life of immorality. God answered the unceasing prayers
of his mother, St. Monica, and in due course, St. Augustine
was baptized. He became the bishop of Hippo, a famous
Catholic writer, and a Father of the Church.[13]

Even the most horrendously wicked people can be
moved by the grace of God and brought to repentance
and conversion. St. Olga (c. 890–969) was an evil prin-
cess from Kiev. When a neighboring tribe killed her husband, she unleashed her revengeful wrath by massacring
the entire tribe, ruthlessly burying alive and burning them
to death. Years later, after a visit to Constantinople, she
was converted to Christianity. She spent the rest of her life
zealously trying to evangelize her people. She did not see

13. *http://www.catholic.org/saints/saint.php?saint_id=418.*

success during her lifetime, but for her devoted efforts, she was proclaimed a saint.[14]

Her grandson, Vladimir (c. 956–1015), was just as nefarious as his grandmother. He was a murderer and a rapist. He had a harem of hundreds of women. He offered human sacrifices. Even still, God's grace changed his heart. Eventually, likely thanks to his grandmother's prayers, Vladimir was baptized. He embraced the Christian faith and dramatically changed his life, first by dismissing his harem and destroying the pagan temple. Then full of zeal, Vladimir worked tirelessly to convert his people. Under his rule, the seeds of faith planted by his grandmother finally bore fruit.[15]

From the lives of St. Olga and St. Vladimir, we can see that the enormity of one's sins can lead a sinner to profoundly appreciate the infinite depths of God's mercy and love. Our Lord himself told a parable to illustrate this lesson:

> "A certain creditor had two debtors; one owed five hundred denarii and the other fifty. When they could not pay, he forgave them both. Now which of them will love him more?" Simon answered, "The one, I suppose, to whom he forgave more." And he said to him, "You have judged rightly."[16]

The keen understanding and intense experience of God's boundless mercy and forgiveness can change the

---

14. Thomas Craughwell, Saints Behaving Badly: The Cutthroats, Crooks, Trollops, Con Men, and Devil-Worshippers Who Became Saints, (New York: Doubleday, 2006), pp. 82–88.

15. Craughwell, pp. 89–94.

16. Lk 7:41–43.

heart of even the most hardened sinner and inflame the soul with love. No wonder so many converts and reverts become champions of the faith! Perhaps this is why God allows certain souls to flounder, fall, and hit rock bottom despite the dedicated efforts and constant prayers of their parents. Although their sins cause him great sorrow, their appeal to his mercy brings great joy because it is very often followed by greater love, as evidenced in Christ's words:

> Just so, I tell you, there will be more joy in heaven over one sinner who repents than over ninety-nine righteous persons who need no repentance.[17]

> And even if the sins of souls were as dark as night, when the sinner turns to My mercy he gives Me the greatest praise and is the glory of My Passion.[18]

If God allows us to go through this crucible of suffering over the precarious state of our children's souls, we must trust that he will use it for their salvation and ours. And so we must pray and wait for God to answer our prayers and bring our children to conversion. United to Christ in his sorrow over unrepentant souls, we can offer up our sufferings in reparation for our sins and the sins of our children. Imitating Christ in his immeasurable mercy, we can be portals of his mercy, offering our children love and forgiveness despite the pain that they cause us.

Above all, we must live with a confident trust and a joyful hope. And our hope must be not only that they will return to their faith, but that when they do, they will come back in humble awe of God's mercy and with hearts on

---

17. Lk 15:7.
18. Kowalska, 378.

fire with ardent love, raring to be apostles, missionaries and evangelists—like St. Mary Magdalen, like St. Paul, like St. Augustine. Even, if need be, like St. Olga and St. Vladimir. Our hope must be that they will be like countless men and women, who, saved from the gates of hell, devotedly show the way to the gates of heaven. With such hope and trust, even in the midst of suffering, we have every reason to rejoice, and to rejoice always.

Rejoice always,
pray constantly,
give thanks in all circumstances;
for this is the will of God in Christ Jesus for you.

— 1 Thessalonians 5:16–18

APPENDIX: Catechetical Resources

> Parents are the first and most important educators of their own children, and they also posses a fundamental competence in this area; they are educators, because they are parents.
>
> — St. Pope John Paul II[1]

Children's prayer of Consecration to Mary

O My Queen, O My Mother,
I give myself to you.
And to show that I love you,
I offer to you this day
my eyes, my ears,
my mouth, my heart,
my body, and my soul.
Therefore, dear Mother,
Since I am your own, keep me and guard me.
Help me to love Jesus more each day.[2]

A Mother's Prayer

O God, you alone really know what a mother's heart is,
  since it was you who created it.
You, only, can understand the immense love a woman has for
  her children.
Protect, I implore you, our children who are yours also.
Keep them in health and shield their souls from all danger.
Make them honest, straightforward, courageous in duty, pure
  and virtuous.

---

1. John Paul II, *Letter to Families*, 2 February 1994, *https://w2.vatican.va/content/john-paul-ii/en/letters/1994/documents/hf_jp-ii_let_02021994_families.html. 16.*

2. Author unknown.

You know, O Father, how delicate is the work of education.

Each child has its own character and needs to be treated for its own good

in a special and well-adapted manner.

Help me to understand each one of my children,

to find the best means of access to their souls so as to effectively help their formation, that they may become men of valor and good Christians.

Grant that I may be tender without weakness and firm without unkindness,

to command with wisdom, and to follow their accomplishments with calm.

Keep me from all nervousness and from all outbreaks of temper,

from all laxity and excessive indulgence.

Place on my lips expedient words of encouragement or words of appropriate reprimand. Grant that I may always enjoy the confidence of my children.

Spare us, Lord, the anguish of seeing them ill and, worse still, that of seeing them go astray.

Keep them on your chosen way for the joy of both of us,

for their ultimate good and for your glory, O our Father in Heaven. Amen.[3]

Preschool and Kindergarten

Gallery, Philip D., and Janet L. Harlow. *Can You Find Saints?* Cincinnati: St. Anthony Messenger Press, 2003.

Kieffer, Jean-François, and Christine Ponsard. *Illustrated Gospel for Children.* New York: Magnificat, 2010.

Maryknoll Sisters. *Catholic Children's Treasure Box, Vol. 1–20.* Charlotte, NC: Tan Press, 1996.

---

3. Author unknown. My mother has said this prayer daily ever since my siblings and I were young. She continues to do so for her grandchildren.

Pinto, Maria da Conceiacao Ferreira. *Let the Children Come to Me: A Reusable, Interactive Poster Set on the Life of Jesus.* Boston: Pauline Books & Media, 2003.

Lower Elementary

A Sister of Notre Dame. *True Stories for First Communicants.* Long Prairie, Minn.: Neumann Press, 2003.

Bennet, Father Kelley. *The New St. Joseph Baltimore Catechism (No. 1).* Second revised edition. Totowa, N.J.: Catholic Book Publishing Corp., 1995.

Bennet, Father Kelley. *The New St. Joseph First Communion Catechism.* Revised edition. Totowa, N.J.: Catholic Book Publishing Corp., 2012.

Encounter the Saints. (Series of Saint Biographies). Boston: Pauline Books and Media.

Faith and Life Series. San Francisco: Ignatius Press, 2011. These are catechism books for grades one through eight.

Hefferman, Anne Eileen, FSP. *57 Stories of Saints.* Boston: Pauline Books, 2006.

Houselander, Carryl. *Catholic Tales for Boys and Girls.* Manchester, N.H.: Sophia Institute Press, 2002.

Johnson, Theresa A. *Rare Catholic Stories.* Little Way Press, 2007.

Lelia, Sister Mary. *Leading the Little Ones to Mary.* New York: Montfort, 1999.

Lovasik, Lawrence G. *The New Catholic Picture Bible.* Totowa, N.J.: Catholic Book Publishing Corp., 1998.

Morrow, Louis LaRavoire. *My First Holy Communion.* Kenosha, Wis.: Our Mission House, Sisters of Mary Immaculate, 2010.

Nicholson, Nancy. Devotional Stories for Little Folks. *Catholic Heritage Curricula,* 2002.

Nicholson, Nancy. Devotional Stories for Little Folks, Too. *AMDG for Little Folks,* 2007.

Pochocki, Ethel. *Around the Year Once Upon a Time Saints.* Bathgate, N.D.: Bethlehem Books, 2009.

Upper Elementary

Bennet, Father Kelley. *The New St. Joseph Baltimore Catechism (No. 2)*. Second revised edition. Totowa, N.J.: Catholic Book Publishing Corp., 1991.

Bliss, Father Geoffrey. *My Path to Heaven: A Young Person's Guide to the Faith*. Manchester, N.H.: Sophia Institute Press, 2005.

Coggi, Father Roberto. *Little Catechism on the Eucharist*. New Hope Publications, 2005.

Faith and Life Series. San Francisco: Ignatius Press, 2011. These are catechism books for grades one through eight.

Daniel-Rops, Henri. *Legend of Young Saints*. Manchester, N.H.: Sophia Institute Press, 2009.

Grispino, Rev. Joseph A., Dr. Samuel Terrien, and Rabbi David H. Wice, eds. *Golden Children's Bible*. Golden Books, 1993.

Lappin, Peter. *Dominic Savio: Teenage Saint*. Roman Catholic Books, 1999. This gem is out of print but is extremely inspiring. Here is a saint to whom modern-day boys can relate!

Loyola, Mother Mary. *King of the Golden City*. Pro Multis Media, 2008.

Maltimore, Father P. Henry. *Heroes of God's Church*. Long Prairie, Minn.: Neumann Press, 2001.

Pinto, Matthew. *Friendly Defenders Catholic Flash Cards*. Ascension Press, 2001. These flash cards teach your children how to defend their faith; they're great for discussion and memorization.

Vision Books Series of Saint Biographies. New York: Ignatius Press.

Wiseman, Nicholas. *Fabiola*. Hillside Education, 2011. Wiseman provides an inspiring account of the young and courageous martyrs of the early church.

Resources for Parents

Bennett, Art and Laraine. *The Temperament God Gave Your Kids*. Huntington, Ind.: Our Sunday Visitor, 2012.

Catechism of the Catholic Church (2nd ed.). Washington, DC: Libreria Editrice Vaticana–United States Conference of Catholic Bishops, 2000.

Chapman, Gary, PhD, and Ross Campbell, MD. *The 5 Love Languages of Children.* Moody Publishers, 2012.

Daughters of St. Paul. *Saint Paul Daily Missal.* Boston: Pauline Books & Media, 2012. This missal contains all the scripture readings and prayers for all Sundays and weekdays, as well as a treasury of prayers.

Isaacs, David. *Character Building: A Guide for Parents and Teachers.* Four Courts Press, 2001.

Smith, Carolyn. *Growing Up in God's Image.* Full Quiver Publishing, 2012. This is a straightforward yet beautiful way to talk about the facts of life with your children.

Johnson, Theresa A. *A Year With God: Celebrating the Liturgical Year.* Little Way Press, 2005. This curriculum provides fun and inspiring family tradition ideas, crafts, and prayers for feast days, Advent, Lent, and Ordinary Time.

Sattler, Father Henry V. *Parents, Children, and the Facts of Life.* Charlotte, N.C.: Tan Books, 1993.

Stenson, James B. *Compass: a Handbook on Parent Leadership.* New York: Scepter, 2003.

Stenson, James B. *Lifeline: The Religious Upbringing of Your Children.* New York: Scepter, 1997.

The Greatest Miracle. Directed Bruce Morris. Arc Entertainment, 2012. DVD, 69 minutes. This beautiful, animated movie about the Holy Mass will encourage you and your children to a more reverent, prayerful participation.

Trese, Leo J. *The Faith Explained.* New Rochelle, NY: Scepter, 2000.

Urteaga, Jues. *God and Children.* Sinag-Tala, 1984.

Internet Resources

10kids.com: This site hosts a wonderful collection of articles and resources on parenting, marriage, and housekeeping by a Catholic mother of ten children.

catholicicing.com: Activities and crafts abound on this internet resource, geared to help you and your family celebrate Advent, Lent, and all the major feast days of the liturgical year.

http://catholicmom.com provides articles, activities, resources, links, and more to help families develop their Catholic faith.

mercyformarthas.com: This is my blog about Catholic homeschooling and family life.

pluggedin.com: Look here for movie ratings with a Christian outlook, provided by Focus on the Family.